Accounting Principles II

By Elizabeth A. Minbiole, CPA, MBA

IDG Books Worldwide, Inc.

An International Data Group Company

Foster City, CA ♦ Chicago, IL ♦ Indianapolis, IN ♦ New York, NY

About the Author

Elizabeth A. Minbiole, CPA, MBA, is an associate professor at Northwood University in Midland, Michigan, where she teaches accounting principles, cost accounting, and financial statement analysis; as well as managerial accounting in the Richard DeVos Graduate School of Management.

Publisher's Acknowledgments
Editorial

Project Editor: Linda Brandon
Acquisitions Editor: Kris Fulkerson
Copy Editor: Rowena Rappaport
Technical Editor: John Tracy, Ph.D., CPA
Editorial Assistant: Melissa Bluhm

Production

Indexer: York Production Services, Inc.
Proofreader: York Production Services, Inc.
IDG Books Indianapolis Production Department

CliffsQuickReview™ Accounting Principles II
Published by
IDG Books Worldwide, Inc.
An International Data Group Company
919 E. Hillsdale Blvd.
Suite 400
Foster City, CA 94404

www.idgbooks.com (IDG Books Worldwide Web site)
www.cliffsnotes.com (CliffsNotes Web site)

Library of Congress Control Number: 00-103368

ISBN: 0-7645-8565-7

Printed in the United States of America

10 9 8 7 6 5 4 3 2 1

1V/RQ/QX/QQ/IN

Distributed in the United States by IDG Books Worldwide, Inc.

Distributed by CDG Books Canada Inc. for Canada; by Transworld Publishers Limited in the United Kingdom; by IDG Norge Books for Norway; by IDG Sweden Books for Sweden; by IDG Books Australia Publishing Corporation Pty. Ltd. for Australia and New Zealand; by TransQuest Publishers Pte Ltd. for Singapore, Malaysia, Thailand, Indonesia, and Hong Kong; by Gotop Information Inc. for Taiwan; by ICG Muse, Inc. for Japan; by Intersoft for South Africa; by Eyrolles for France; by International Thomson Publishing for Germany, Austria and Switzerland; by Distribuidora Cuspide for Argentina; by LR International for Brazil; by Galileo Libros for Chile; by Ediciones ZETA S.C.R. Ltda. for Peru; by WS Computer Publishing Corporation, Inc., for the Philippines; by Contemporanea de Ediciones for Venezuela; by Express Computer Distributors for the Caribbean and West Indies; by Micronesia Media Distributor, Inc. for Micronesia; by Chips Computadoras S.A. de C.V. for Mexico; by Editorial Norma de Panama S.A. for Panama; by American Bookshops for Finland.

For general information on IDG Books Worldwide's books in the U.S., please call our Consumer Customer Service department at **800-762-2974.** For reseller information, including discounts and premium sales, please call our Reseller Customer Service department at **800-434-3422.**

For information on where to purchase IDG Books Worldwide's books outside the U.S., please contact our International Sales department at **317-596-5530** or fax **317-572-4002.**

For consumer information on foreign language translations, please contact our Customer Service department at **1-800-434-3422**, fax 317-572-4002, or e-mail rights@idgbooks.com.

For information on licensing foreign or domestic rights, please phone **650-653-7098.**

For sales inquiries and special prices for bulk quantities, please contact our Order Services department at **800-434-3422** or write to the address above.

For information on using IDG Books Worldwide's books in the classroom or for ordering examination copies, please contact our Educational Sales department at **800-434-2086** or fax **317-572-4005.**

For press review copies, author interviews, or other publicity information, please contact our Public Relations department at **650-653-7000** or fax **650-653-7500.**

For authorization to photocopy items for corporate, personal, or educational use, please contact Copyright Clearance Center, 222 Rosewood Drive, Danvers, MA 01923, or fax **978-750-4470.**

CONTENTS

FUNDAMENTAL IDEAS

For the purpose of this review, your knowledge of the following fundamental ideas is assumed:

- Generally accepted accounting principles: accrual basis of accounting, revenue recognition principle, matching principle, time period assumption, materiality principle.

- Financial statements: balance sheet, income statement, statement of owners' equity.

- Analyzing transactions

- Account

- Contra account

- Journal

- Journal entry

- General ledger

- Accounts receivable

- Reserve account

- Allowance for doubtful accounts

- Inventory systems: perpetual inventory, periodic inventory.

- Inventory costing methods: FIFO, LIFO.

- Cost of goods sold

- Gross profit

- Depreciation: straight-line depreciation.

- Compounding

If you feel that you are weak in any of these topics, you should refer to *CliffsQuickReview Accounting Principles I.*

A **liability** is an existing debt or obligation of a company. It is an amount owed to a third-party creditor that requires something of value, usually cash, to be transferred to the creditor to settle the debt. Most obligations are known amounts based on invoices and contracts; some liabilities are estimated because the value that changes hands is not fixed at the time of the initial transaction. Liabilities are reported in the balance sheet as current (short-term) or long-term (see Chapter 2), based on when they are due to be paid. Current liabilities are those obligations that will be paid within the next year.

Accounts Payable

Accounts payable represent trade payables, those obligations that exist based on the good faith credit of the business or owner and for which a formal note has not been signed. Purchases of merchandise or supplies on an account are examples of liabilities recorded as accounts payable. The credit terms of each transaction and the company's ability to take advantage of available discounts determine the timing of payments of accounts payable balances.

Payroll Liabilities

Amounts owed to employees for work performed are recorded separately from accounts payable. Expense accounts such as salaries or wages expense are used to record an employee's gross earnings and a liability account such as salaries payable, wages payable, or accrued wages payable is used to record the net pay obligation to employees. Additional payroll-related liabilities include amounts owed to third parties for any amounts withheld from the gross earnings of each employee and the payroll taxes owed by the employer. Examples of withholdings from gross earnings include federal, state, and local income taxes and FICA (Federal Insurance Contributions Act: social security and medical) taxes, investments in retirement and savings accounts, health-care premiums, union dues, uniforms, alimony, child care, loan payments, stock purchase plans offered by employer, and charitable contributions. The employer payroll taxes include social security and medical taxes (same amount as employees), federal unemployment tax, and state unemployment tax.

Net pay and withholding liabilities

Payroll withholdings include required and voluntary deductions authorized by each employee. Withheld amounts represent liabilities, as the company must pay the amounts withheld to the appropriate third party. The amounts do not represent expenses of the employer. The employer is simply acting as an intermediary, collecting money from employees and passing it on to third parties.

Required deductions. These deductions are made for federal income taxes, and when applicable, state and local income taxes. The amounts withheld are based on an employee's earnings and designated **withholding allowances.** Withholding allowances are usually based on the number of exemptions an employee will claim on his/her income tax return, but may be adjusted based on the employee's estimated income tax liability. The employee is required to complete a W-4 form authorizing the number of withholdings before the employer can process payroll. The employer withholds income tax amounts based on the allowances designated by each employee and tax tables provided by the government. The employer pays these withheld amounts to the Internal Revenue Service (IRS). In addition to income taxes, FICA requires a deduction from employees' pay for federal social security and Medicare benefits programs. This deduction is usually referred to as FICA taxes. Although recently the tax percentage has not changed, the amount of wages on which an employee pays the social security portion of the tax has been changing yearly. Currently, the social security tax rate is 6.2% of earnings up to a specific amount—for 2000, the amount is $76,200. The Medicare tax rate is 1.45% and is paid on all earnings regardless of the amount. FICA taxes are withheld by the employer and are deposited along with federal income taxes in a financial institution.

Voluntary deductions. These deductions are authorized by employees and may include amounts for purchase of company stock, retirement investments, deposits in a savings account, loan payments, union dues, charitable contributions, health, dental, and life insurance premiums, and alimony.

Net pay. Net pay is the employee's gross earnings less mandatory and voluntary deductions. It is the amount the employee receives on payday, so called "take-home pay." An entry to record a payroll accrual includes an increase (debit) to wages expense for the gross earnings of employees, increases (credits) to separate accounts for each type of withholding liability, and an increase (credit) to a payroll liability account, such as wages payable, for employees' net pay.

Special journals are used for certain transactions. However, all companies use a general journal. In this book, all journal entries will be shown in the general journal format.

General Journal

Date	Account Title and Description	Ref.	Debit	Credit
20X0				
Feb. 28	Wages Expense		3,268	
	FICA Taxes Payable (7.65% × $3,268)			250
	Federal Income Taxes Payable (table)			350
	State Income Taxes Payable (table)			120
	Health Insurance Premiums Payable			80
	Union Dues Payable			50
	Wages Payable			2,418
	To accrue 2/28 payroll			

When the employees are paid, an entry is made to reduce (debit) the wages payable account balance and decrease (credit) cash.

General Journal

Date	Account Title and Description	Ref.	Debit	Credit
20X0				
Feb. 28	Wages Payable		2,418	
	Cash			2,418
	Payment of payroll for 2/28			

Employer payroll taxes

The employer is responsible for three payroll-related taxes:

- FICA Taxes.

- Federal Unemployment Taxes (FUTA).

- State Unemployment Taxes (SUTA).

The FICA taxes paid by the employers are an amount equal to the FICA taxes paid by the employees. Currently, FUTA taxes are 6.2% of the first $9,000 earned by each employee. Because unemployment taxes are a joint federal and state program, a credit of 5.4% is allowed by the federal government for unemployment taxes paid to the state. This often results in a 0.8% federal unemployment tax rate. In most states, state unemployment taxes are 5.4% of the first $9,000 earned by each employee. States may reduce this rate for employers with a history of creating little unemployment. Higher turnover and seasonal hiring may increase the rate.

The entry for the employer's payroll taxes expense for the Feb. 28th payroll would include increases (credits) to liabilities for FICA taxes of $250 (the employer has to match the amount paid by employees), FUTA taxes of $26 (0.8% × $3,268), and SUTA taxes of $176 (5.4% × $3,268). The amount of the increase (debit) to payroll tax expense is determined by adding the amounts of the three liabilities.

General Journal

Date	Account Title and Description	Ref.	Debit	Credit
20X0				
Feb. 28	Payroll Tax Expense		452	
	FICA Taxes Payable (7.65% × $3,268)			250
	Federal Unemployment Taxes Payable (0.8% × $3,268)			26
	State Unemployment Taxes Payable (5.4% × $3,268)			176
	To accrue employer's payroll taxes			

Notes Payable

A liability is created when a company signs a note for the purpose of borrowing money or extending its payment period credit. A note may be signed for an overdue invoice when the company needs to extend its payment, when the company borrows cash, or in exchange for an asset. An extension of the normal credit period for paying amounts owed often requires that a company sign a note, resulting in a transfer of the liability from accounts payable to notes payable. Notes payable are classified as current liabilities when the amounts are due within one year of the balance sheet date. When the debt is long-term (payable after one year) but requires a payment within the twelve-month period following the balance sheet date, the amount of the payment is classified as a current liability in the balance sheet. The portion of the debt to be paid after one year is classified as a long-term liability.

Notes payable almost always require interest payments. The interest owed for the period the debt has been outstanding that has not been paid must be accrued. Accruing interest creates an expense and a liability. A different liability account is used for interest payable so it can be separately identified. The entries for a six-month, $12,000 note, signed November 1 by The Quality Control Corp., with interest at 10% are:

General Journal

Date	Account Title and Description	Ref.	Debit	Credit
20X0				
Nov.1	Cash		12,000	
	Notes Payable			12,000
	To record borrowing			
Dec. 31	Interest Expense		200	
	Interest Payable			200
	To accrue interest for two months ($12,000 × 10% × 2/12)			
20X1				
Apr. 30	Notes Payable		12,000	
	Interest Payable		200	
	Interest Expense (4 months)		400	
	Cash			12,600
	To record payment of note with interest			

If The Quality Control Corp. signs a note for $12,000 including interest, it is called a noninterest-bearing note because the $12,000 represents the total amount due at maturity and not the amount of cash received by The Quality Control Corp. Interest must be calculated (imputed) using an estimate of the interest rate at which the company could have borrowed and the present value tables (see Appendix A and B). The present value of the note on the day of signing represents the amount of cash received by the borrower. The total interest expense (cost of borrowing) is the difference between the present value of the note and the maturity value of the note. In order to follow the matching principle, the total interest expense is initially recorded as "Discount on Notes Payable." Over the term of the note, the discount balance is charged to (amortized) interest expense such that at maturity of the note, the balance in the discount account is zero. Discount on notes payable is a contra account used to value the Notes Payable shown in the balance sheet.

Unearned revenues
Unearned revenues represent amounts paid in advance by the customer for an exchange of goods or services. Examples of unearned revenues are deposits, subscriptions for magazines or newspapers paid in advance, airline tickets paid in advance of flying, and season tickets to sporting and entertainment events. As the cash is received, the cash account is increased (debited) and unearned revenue, a liability account, is increased (credited). As the seller of the product or service earns the revenue by providing the goods or services, the unearned revenues account is decreased (debited) and revenues are increased (credited). Unearned revenues are classified as current or long-term liabilities based on when the product or service is expected to be delivered to the customer.

Contingent liabilities

A **contingent liability** represents a potential future liability based on actions already taken by a company. Lawsuits, product warranties, debt guarantees, and IRS disputes are examples of contingent liabilities. The guidelines to follow in determining whether a contingent liability must be recorded as a liability or just disclosed in financial statements are as follows:

- Record a liability if the contingency is likely to occur, or is probable and can be reasonably estimated (for example, product warranty costs).

- Disclose in notes to financial statements if the contingency is reasonably possible (for example, legal suits, debt guarantees, and IRS disputes that may require a cash settlement or otherwise impact financial statements).

- Do nothing if the contingency is unlikely to occur, or remote (for example, legal suits, debt guarantees, and IRS disputes the company believes it will win).

Warranty liabilities

A warranty represents an obligation of the selling company to repair or replace defective products for a certain period of time. This obligation meets the probable and reasonably estimated criteria of a contingent liability because a company's prior history of making warranty repairs identifies warranty work as probable, and current warranty costs can be reasonably estimated based on past work and current warranties. This obligation creates an expense that is matched against the revenues in the current period's income statement (matching principle) and an estimated liability. The liability is estimated because although the company knows it will have to do warranty work, they do not know the exact cost of that work. If Oxy Co. sells 10,000 units, expecting 1% to be returned under warranty and an average cost of $50 to repair each unit, the estimated liability of $5,000 (10,000 × 1% × $50) is recorded as follows:

General Journal

Date	Account Title and Description	Ref.	Debit	Credit
20X0				
May 31	Warranty Expense		5,000	
	Estimated Warranty Payable			5,000
	To record warranty for May sales			

When warranty work is performed, the estimated warranty payable is decreased.

Long-term liabilities are existing obligations or debts due after one year or operating cycle, whichever is longer. They appear on the balance sheet after total current liabilities and before owners' equity. Examples of long-term liabilities are notes payable, mortgage payable, obligations under long-term capital leases, bonds payable, pension and other post-employment benefit obligations, and deferred income taxes. The values of many long-term liabilities represent the present value of the anticipated future cash outflows. Present value represents the amount that should be invested now, given a specific interest rate, to accumulate to a future amount.

Notes Payable

Notes payable represent obligations to banks or other creditors based on formal written agreements. A specific interest rate is usually identified in the agreement. Following the matching principle, if interest is owed but has not been paid, it is accrued prior to the preparation of the financial statements. Assume The Flower Lady signed a $10,000 three-year note with interest of 10% on July 1 in exchange for a piece of equipment. The interest is due and payable quarterly on Oct.1, Jan. 1, April 1, and July 1. The Flower Lady operates on a calendar-year basis and issues financial statements at the end of each quarter. A long-term note payable must be recorded as of July 1 with interest accrued at the end of each quarter. The entries related to the note for the current year are:

General Journal

Date	Account Title and Description	Ref.	Debit	Credit
20X0				
July 1	Equipment		10,000	
	Notes Payable			10,000
	To finance purchase of equipment			
Sept. 30	Interest Expense ($10,000 × 10% × $^3/_{12}$)		250	
	Interest Payable			250
	To accrue 3rd quarter interest			
Oct. 1	Interest Payable		250	
	Cash			250
	To pay interest			
Dec. 31	Interest Expense ($10,000 × 10% × $^3/_{12}$)		250	
	Interest Payable			250
	To accrue 4th quarter interest			

In the final year, the June 30 quarterly interest accrual and July 1 payoff would be as shown.

General Journal

Date	Account Title and Description	Ref.	Debit	Credit
20X3				
June 30	Interest Expense ($10,000 × 10% × $^3/_{12}$)		250	
	Interest Payable			250
	To accrue 2nd quarter interest			
July 1	Notes Payable		10,000	
	Interest Payable		250	
	Cash			10,250
	To pay off note and interest due			

If interest is not paid until maturity of the note, the amount of interest accrued is often determined by compounding. The annual interest expense is the beginning of the year note principal plus accrued interest payable times the annual interest rate. Generally, it is assumed that in any arm's length transaction, the interest rate stated on a note signed in exchange for goods and services is a fair rate. If an interest rate is not stated, the exchange value is based on the value of the goods or services received. The difference between the exchange value and the face amount of the note signed is considered interest.

20|45318

Mortgage Payable

The long-term financing used to purchase property is called a mortgage. The property itself serves as collateral for the mortgage until it is paid off. A mortgage usually requires equal payments, consisting of principal and interest, throughout its term. The early payments consist of more interest than principal. Over the life of the mortgage, the portion of each payment that represents principal increases and the interest portion decreases. This decrease occurs because interest is calculated on the outstanding principal balance that declines as payments are made.

The Stats Man obtains a fifteen-year $175,000 mortgage with a 7.5% interest rate and a monthly payment of $1,622.28. The borrowing and receipt of cash is recorded with an increase (debit) to cash and an increase (credit) to mortgage payable. When a payment is made, mortgage payable is decreased (debited) for the principal portion of the payment, interest expense is increased (debited) for the interest portion of the payment, and cash is decreased (credited) by the payment amount of $1,622.28. The interest portion of the first payment is $1,093.75, which is calculated by multiplying the $175,000 principal balance times the 7.5% interest rate times $\frac{1}{12}$ because payments are made monthly. The interest portion of the second payment is $1,090.45. It is different from the first payment because after the first payment, the outstanding principal balance was reduced by $528.53, the difference between the payment amount of $1,622.28 and the $1,093.75 interest expense. The $1,090.45 was calculated by multiplying the $174,471.47 principal balance times 7.5% times $\frac{1}{12}$. This process of calculating the interest portion of each payment continues until the mortgage is paid off. The principal portion of each payment is the difference between the cash paid and the interest expense calculated. The entries to record the receipt of the mortgage and the first two installment payments are:

General Journal

Date	Account Title and Description	Ref.	Debit	Credit
20X4				
Apr.1	Cash		175,000.00	
	Mortgage Payable			175,000.00
	Obtained mortgage			
May 1	Mortgage Payable		528.53	
	Interest Expense ($175,000 \times 7.5\% \times \frac{1}{12}$)		1,093.75	
	Cash			1622.28
	First mortgage installment			
June 1	Mortgage Payable		531.83	
	Interest Expense (($175,000 - 528.53) \times 7.5\% \times \frac{1}{12}$)		1,090.45	
	Cash			1,622.28
	Second mortgage installment			

Lease Obligations

In a lease, the property owner (lessor) gives the right to use property to a third party (lessee) in exchange for a series of rental payments. The accounting for lease obligations is determined based on the substance of the transaction. Leases are categorized as operating or capital leases using the following four questions which are simplified from the criteria established in Statement of Financial Accounting Standards No. 13, Accounting for Leases, issued in 1976 by the Financial Accounting Standards Board (FASB):

- Does the title pass to the lessee at any time during or at the end of the lease?

- Is there an opportunity to purchase the leased item at the end of the lease term at a price so below market rate (a bargain purchase option) that the lessee is likely to take advantage of the opportunity?

- Is the term of the lease greater than or equal to 75% of the service life of the leased item?

- At the time of the agreement, is the present value of the minimum lease payments greater than or equal to 90% of the fair value of the leased item to the lessor?

If the answer to any *one* of these is yes, the lease is considered a capital lease because the lessee has in essence accepted the risks and benefits of ownership. A capital lease requires an asset, which must be subsequently depreciated, and a liability to be recorded based on the value of the asset on the date of the lease. The liability is usually paid off with a series of equal payments. A portion of each payment is interest, similar to the mortgage payments previously discussed.

If the questions are all answered no, the lease is considered an operating lease and recorded as lease or rent expense, an income statement account, every time a payment is made.

Bonds Payable

One source of financing available to corporations is long-term bonds. Bonds represent an obligation to repay a principal amount at a future date and pay interest, usually on a semi-annual basis. Unlike notes payable, which normally represent an amount owed to one lender, a large number of bonds are normally issued at the same time to different lenders. These lenders, also known as investors, may sell their bonds to another investor prior to their maturity.

Types of bonds

There are many different types of bonds available to interested investors. Some of the more common forms are:

- **Serial bonds.** Bonds issued in groups that mature at different dates. For example, $5,000,000 of serial bonds, $500,000 of which mature each year from 5–14 years after they are issued.

- **Sinking fund bonds.** Bonds that require the issuer to set aside a pool of assets used only to repay the bonds at maturity. These bonds reduce the risk that the company will not have enough cash to repay the bonds at maturity.

- **Convertible bonds.** Bonds that can be exchanged for a fixed number of shares of the company's common stock. In most cases, it is the investor's decision to convert the bonds to stock, although certain types of convertible bonds allow the issuing company to determine if and when bonds are converted.

- **Registered bonds.** Bonds issued in the name of a specific owner. This is how most bonds are issued today. Having a registered bond allows the owner to automatically receive the interest payments when they are made.

- **Bearer bonds.** Bonds that require the bondholder, also called the bearer, to go to a bank or broker with the bond or coupons attached to the bond to receive the interest and principal payments. They are called bearer or coupon bonds because the person presenting the bond or coupon receives the interest and principal payments.

- **Secured bonds.** Bonds are secured when specific company assets are pledged to serve as collateral for the bondholders. If the company fails to make payments according to the bond terms, the owners of secured bonds may require the assets to be sold to generate cash for the payments.

- **Debenture bonds.** These unsecured bonds require the bondholders to rely on the good name and financial stability of the issuing company for repayment of principal and interest amounts. These bonds are usually riskier than secured bonds. A subordinated debenture bond means the bond is repaid after other unsecured debt, as noted in the bond agreement.

Bond prices

The price of a bond is based on the market's assessment of any risk associated with the company that issues (sells) the bonds. The higher the risk associated with the company, the higher the interest rate. Bonds issued with a **coupon interest rate** (also called contract rate or stated rate) higher than the market interest rate are said to be offered at a **premium**. The premium is necessary to compensate the bond purchaser for the above average risk being assumed. Bonds are issued at a **discount** when the coupon interest rate is below the market interest rate. Bonds sold at a discount result in a company receiving less cash than the face value of the bonds.

Bonds are denominated in $1,000s. A market price of 100 means the bond sold for 100% of face value. If its face value is $1,000, the sales price was $1,000. A bond sold at 102, a premium, would generate $1,020 cash for the issuing company (102% × $1,000) while one sold at 97, a discount, would provide $970 cash for the issuing company (97% × $1,000).

To illustrate how bond pricing works, assume Lighting Process, Inc. issued $10,000 of ten-year bonds with a coupon interest rate of 10% and semi-annual interest payments when the market interest rate is 10%. This means Lighting Process, Inc. will repay the principal amount of $10,000 at maturity in ten years and will pay $500 interest ($10,000 × 10% coupon interest rate × $\frac{6}{12}$) every six months. The price of the bonds is based on the present value of these future cash flows. The principal and interest amounts are based on the face amounts of the bond while the present value factors used to calculate the value of the bond at issuance are based on the market interest rate of 10%. Given these facts, the purchaser would be willing to pay $10,000, or the face value of the bond, as both the coupon interest rate and the market interest rate were the same. The total cash paid to investors over the life of the bonds is $20,000, $10,000 of principal at maturity and $10,000 ($500 × 20 periods) in interest throughout the life of the bonds.

Present Value of Bond Sold at Market Interest Rate

	Cash Flows	Present Value Factor	Present Value
Principal Payment	$10,000	.3769[1]	$ 3,769
Interest Payments	500	12.4622[2]	6,231
Price of Bond			$10,000

[1] Present value of 1 using 5% (10% annual coupon interest rate times $\frac{6}{12}$) and 20 periods (10-year bonds times 2 interest payments per year) from Appendix A.

[2] Present value of annuity of 1 using 5% and 20 periods from Appendix B.

Assume instead that Lighting Process, Inc. issued bonds with a coupon rate of 9% when the market rate was 10%. The bond purchaser would be willing to pay only $9,377 because Lighting Process, Inc. will pay $450 in interest every six months ($10,000 × 9% × $^6/_{12}$), which is lower than the market rate of interest of $500 every six months. The total cash paid to investors over the life of the bonds is $19,000, $10,000 of principal at maturity and $9,000 ($450 × 20 periods) in interest throughout the life of the bonds.

Present Value of Bond Sold Below Market Interest Rate

	Cash Flows	*Present Value Factor*	*Present Value*
Principal Payment	$10,000	.3769 [1]	$3,769
Interest Payments	450	12.4622 [2]	5,608
Price of Bond			$9,377

[1] Present value of 1 using 5% (10% annual coupon interest rate times $^6/_{12}$) and 20 periods (10-year bonds times 2 interest payments per year) from Appendix A.

[2] Present value of annuity of 1 using 5% and 20 periods from Appendix B.

If instead, Lighting Process, Inc. issued its $10,000 bonds with a coupon rate of 12% when the market rate was 10%, the purchasers would be willing to pay $11,246. Semi-annual interest payments of $600 are calculated using the coupon interest rate of 12% ($10,000 × 12% × $^6/_{12}$). The total cash paid to investors over the life of the bonds is $22,000, $10,000 of principal at maturity and $12,000 ($600 × 20 periods) in interest throughout the life of the bonds. Lighting Process, Inc. receives a premium (more cash than the principal amount) from the purchasers. The purchasers are willing to pay more for the bonds because the purchasers will receive interest payments of $600 when the market interest payment on the bonds was only $500.

Present Value of Bond Sold Above Market Interest Rate

	Cash Flows	Present Value Factor	Present Value
Principal Payment	$10,000	.3769 [(1)]	$ 3,769
Interest Payments	600	12.4622 [(2)]	7,477
Price of Bond			$ 11,246

[(1)] Present value of 1 using 5% (10% annual coupon interest rate × $\%12$) and 20 periods (10-year bonds times 2 interest payments per year) from Appendix A.

[(2)] Present value of annuity of 1 using 5% and 20 periods from Appendix B.

Bonds issued at par

The journal entries made by Lighting Process, Inc. to record its issuance at par of $10,000 ten-year bonds with a coupon rate of 10% and the semiannual interest payments made on June 30 and December 31 are as shown.

General Journal

Date	Account Title and Description	Ref.	Debit	Credit
20X1				
July 1	Cash		10,000	
	Bonds Payable			10,000
	Issued bonds at par			

Date	Account Title and Description	Ref.	Debit	Credit
Dec. 31	Interest Expense ($10,000 × 10% × $1/12$)		500	
	Cash			500
	Semiannual interest payment*			
20X2				
June 30	Interest Expense ($10,000 × 10% × $1/12$)		500	
	Cash			500
	Semiannual interest payment*			

* Assumes no adjusting entries to accrue interest were made on a monthly or quarterly basis as no formal financial statements were prepared.

The bonds are classified as long-term liabilities when they are issued. When the bond matures, the principal repayment is recorded as follows:

General Journal

Date	Account Title and Description	Ref.	Debit	Credit
July 1	Bonds Payable		10,000	
	Cash			10,000
	Paid off bonds at maturity			

Bonds issued at a discount

Lighting Process, Inc. issues $10,000 ten-year bonds, with a coupon interest rate of 9% and semiannual interest payments payable on June 30 and Dec. 31, issued on July 1 when the market interest rate is 10%. The entry to record the issuance of the bonds increases (debits) cash for the $9,377 received, increases (debits) discount on bonds payable for $623, and increases (credits) bonds payable for the $10,000 maturity amount. Discount on bonds payable is a contra account to bonds payable that decreases the value of the bonds and is subtracted from the bonds payable in the long-term liability section of the balance sheet. Initially it is the difference between the cash received and the maturity value of the bond.

General Journal

Date	Account Title and Description	Ref.	Debit	Credit
20X1				
July 1	Cash		9,377	
	Discount on Bonds Payable		623	
	Bonds Payable			10,000
	Issue bonds at a discount			

After this entry, the bond would be included in the long-term liability section of the balance sheet as follows:

Long-term liabilities

Bonds Payable	10,000	
Less: Discount on Bonds Payable	(623)	9,377

The $9,377 is called the **carrying amount** of the bond. The discount on bonds payable is the difference between the cash received and the maturity value of the bonds and represents additional interest expense to Lighting Process, Inc. (the company that issued the bond). The total interest expense can be calculated using the bond-related payments and receipts as shown:

Repayments

Principal	$10,000
Interest ($450 times 20 semiannual periods)	9,000
Total cash payments to investors	19,000
Less: Cash receipts from investors	(9,377)
Total interest expense	$ 9,623

The interest expense is amortized over the twenty periods during which interest is paid. Amortization of the discount may be done using the straight-line or the effective interest method. Currently, generally accepted accounting principles require use of the effective interest method of amortization unless the results under the two methods are not significantly different. If the amounts of interest expense are similar under the two methods, the straight-line method may be used.

The **straight-line method** of allocating the discount to interest expense (also called **amortization** of the discount) spreads the $623 of discount evenly over the 20 semiannual interest payments made for the bonds. To calculate the additional interest expense to be recognized when recording the semiannual interest payments, divide the total discount by the number of interest payments. In this example, an additional $31.15 ($623 ÷ 20) of interest expense would be recognized every six months. This has been rounded to $31 for illustration purposes. The amount of discount amortized ($31) is added to the interest paid ($450) to determine the total interest expense recorded. The entry to pay interest on December 31, 20X1 would be:

General Journal

Date	Account Title and Description	Ref.	Debit	Credit
Dec. 31	Interest Expense		481	
	Discount on Bonds Payable ($623 ÷ 20)			31
	Cash ($10,000 × 9% × $^{6}/_{12}$)			450
	Pay semiannual interest using straight-line amortization			

After the payment is recorded, the carrying value of the bonds payable on the balance sheet increases to $9,408 because the discount has decreased to $592 ($623 – $31).

Long-term liabilities

Bonds Payable   10,000

Less: Discount on Bonds Payable   (592)   9,408

The carrying value will continue to increase as the discount balance decreases with amortization. When the bond matures, the discount will be zero and the bond's carrying value will be the same as its principal amount. The discount amortized for the last payment may be slightly different based on rounding. See Table 2-1 for interest expense calculated using the straight-line method of amortization and carrying value calculations over the life of the bond. At maturity, the entry to record the principal payment is shown in the General Journal entry that follows Table 2-1.

Table 2-1: Straight-Line Amortization of Discount

Date	Beginning Carrying Value (1)	Interest Payment (2)	Discount Amortized (3)	Total Interest Expense (4)=(2)+(3)	Beginning Discount (5)	Ending Discount (6)=(5)-(3)	Ending Carrying Value (7)=(1)+(3)
7/1/X0 (A)	9,377						
12/31/X0	9,377	450	31	481	623	592	9,408
6/30/X1	9,408	450	31	481	592	561	9,439
12/31/X1	9,439	450	31	481	561	530	9,470
6/30/X2	9,470	450	31	481	530	499	9,501
12/31/X2	9,501	450	31	481	499	468	9,532
6/30/X3	9,532	450	31	481	468	437	9,563
12/31/X3	9,563	450	31	481	437	406	9,594
6/30/X4	9,594	450	31	481	406	375	9,625
12/31/X4	9,625	450	31	481	375	344	9,656
6/30/X5	9,656	450	31	481	344	313	9,687
12/31/X5	9,687	450	31	481	313	282	9,718
6/30/X6	9,718	450	31	481	282	251	9,749

Date	Beginning Carrying Value (1)	Interest Payment (2)	Discount Amortized (3)	Total Interest Expense (4)=(2)+(3)	Beginning Discount (5)	Ending Discount (6)=(5)-(3)	Ending Carrying Value (7)=(1)+(3)
12/31/X6	9,749	450	31	481	251	220	9,780
6/30/X7	9,780	450	31	481	220	189	9,811
12/31/X7	9,811	450	31	481	189	158	9,842
6/30/X8	9,842	450	31	481	158	127	9,873
12/31/X8	9,873	450	31	481	127	96	9,904
6/30/X9	9,904	450	31	481	96	65	9,935
12/31/X9	9,935	450	31	481	65	34	9,966
6/30/X10	9,966	450	*34	484	34	0	10,000
		9,000	623	9,623			

* Due to rounding.

(A) At issue, carrying value = $10,000 face value – $623 discount.

General Journal

Date	Account Title and Description	Ref.	Debit	Credit
July 1	Bonds Payable		10,000	
	Cash			10,000
	Repay bond principal at maturity			

The effective interest method of amortizing the discount to interest expense calculates the interest expense using the carrying value of the bonds and the market rate of interest at the time the bonds were issued. For the first interest payment, the interest expense is $469 ($9,377 carrying value × 10% market interest rate × $\frac{6}{12}$ semiannual interest). The semiannual interest paid to bondholders on Dec. 31 is $450 ($10,000 maturity amount of bond × 9% coupon interest rate × $\frac{6}{12}$ for semiannual payment). The $19 difference between the $469 interest expense and the $450 cash payment is the amount of the discount amortized. The entry on December 31 to record the interest payment using the effective interest method of amortizing interest is shown on the following page.

General Journal

Date	Account Title and Descriptiont	Ref.	Debit	Credit
Dec. 31	Interest Expense ($9,377 \times 10\% \times \frac{6}{12}$)		469	
	Discount on Bonds Payable			19
	Cash ($10,000 \times 9\% \times \frac{6}{12}$)			450
	Pay semiannual interest using interest method of amortization			

As the discount is amortized, the discount on bonds payable account's balance decreases and the carrying value of the bond increases. The amount of discount amortized for the last payment is equal to the balance in the discount on bonds payable account. As with the straight-line method of amortization, at the maturity of the bonds, the discount account's balance will be zero and the bond's carrying value will be the same as its principal amount. See Table 2-2 for interest expense and carrying values over the life of the bond calculated using the effective interest method of amortization.

Table 2-2: Interest Method of Amortization of Discount

Date	Beginning Carrying Value (1)	Interest Expense (2)	Interest Payment (3)	Discount Amortized (4)=(2)-(3)	Beginning Discount (5)	Ending Discount (6)=(5)-(4)	Ending Carrying Value (7)=(1)+(3)
7/1/X0 (A)	9,377						
12/31/X0	9,377	469	450	19	623	604	9,396
6/30/X1	9,396	470	450	20	601	584	9,416
12/31/X1	9,416	471	450	21	584	563	9,437
6/30/X2	9,437	472	450	22	563	541	9,459
12/31/X2	9,459	473	450	23	541	518	9,482
6/30/X3	9,482	474	450	24	518	494	9,506
12/31/X3	9,506	475	450	25	494	469	9,531
6/30/X4	9,531	477	450	27	469	442	9,558
12/31/X4	9,558	478	450	28	442	414	9,586
6/30/X5	9,586	479	450	29	414	385	9,615
12/31/X5	9,615	481	450	31	385	354	9,646

Date	Beginning Carrying Value (1)	Interest Expense (2)	Interest Payment (3)	Discount Amortized (4)=(2)-(3)	Beginning Discount (5)	Ending Discount (6)=(5)-(4)	Ending Carrying Value (7)=(1)+(4)
6/30/X6	9,646	482	450	32	354	322	9,678
12/31/X6	9,678	484	450	34	322	288	9,712
6/30/X7	9,712	486	450	36	288	252	9,748
12/31/X7	9,748	487	450	37	252	215	9,785
6/30/X8	9,785	489	450	39	215	176	9,824
12/31/X8	9,824	491	450	41	176	135	9,865
6/30/X9	9,865	493	450	43	135	92	9,908
12/31/X9	9,908	495	450	45	92	47	9,953
6/30/X10	9,953	497	450	*47	47	0	10,000
		9,623	9,000	623			

* Due to rounding.

(A) At issue, carrying value = $10,000 face value – $623 discount.

Bonds issued at a premium

On July 1, Lighting Process, Inc. issues $10,000 ten-year bonds, with a coupon rate of interest of 12% and semiannual interest payments payable on June 30 and December 31, when the market interest rate is 10%. The entry to record the issuance of the bonds increases (debits) cash for the $11,246 received, increases (credits) bonds payable for the $10,000 maturity amount, and increases (credits) premium on bonds payable for $1,246. Premium on bonds payable is a contra account to bonds payable that increases its value and is added to bonds payable in the long-term liability section of the balance sheet.

General Journal

Date	Account Title and Description	Ref.	Debit	Credit
20X1				
July 1	Cash		11,246	
	Bonds Payable			10,000
	Premium on Bonds Payable			1,246
	Issue bonds at a premium			

After the entry, the bonds would be included in the long-term liability section of the balance sheet as follows:

Long-term liabilities

Bonds Payable	10,000	
Plus: Premium on Bonds Payable	1,246	11,246

The premium account balance represents the difference (excess) between the cash received and the principal amount of the bonds. The premium account balance of $1,246 is amortized against interest expense over the twenty interest periods. Unlike the discount that results in additional interest expense when it is amortized, the amortization of premium decreases interest expense. The total interest expense on these bonds will be $10,754 rather than the $12,000 that will be paid in cash.

Repayments

Principal	$10,000
Interest ($600 times 20 semiannual periods)	12,000
Total cash payments to investors	22,000
Less: Cash receipts from investors	(11,246)
Total interest expense	$10,754

As with discount amortization, the amortization of premium may be done using the straight-line or effective interest method. The *straight-line method* spreads the $1,246 premium account's balance evenly over the 20 semiannual interest payments made for the bonds. This method divides the total premium by the number of interest payments to determine the reduction in interest expense to be recognized semiannually. In this case, interest expense will be reduced by $62.30 ($1,246 ÷ 20), say $62, every six months. The entry for the first interest payment would be as follows:

General Journal

Date	Account Title and Description	Ref.	Debit	Credit
Dec. 31	Interest Expense		538	
	Premium on Bonds Payable ($11,246 ÷ 20)		62	
	Cash ($10,000 × 12% × $^{6}/_{12}$)			600
	Pay semiannual interest (using straight-line amortization)			

The carrying value will continue to decrease as the premium account's balance decreases. When the bond matures, the premium account's balance will be zero and the bond's carrying value will be the same as the bond's principal amount. The premium amortized for the last payment should be the balance in the premium on bonds payable account. At maturity, the entry to record the principal repayment is:

General Journal

Date	Account Title and Description	Ref.	Debit	Credit
July 1	Bonds Payable		10,000	
	Cash			10,000
	Repay bond principal at maturity			

See Table 2-3 for interest expense and carrying value calculations over the life of the bond using the straight-line method of amortization.

Table 2-3:

Straight-Line Amortization of Premium

Date	Beginning Carrying Value (1)	Interest Payment (2)	Premium Amortized (3)	Total Interest Expense (4)=(2)-(3)	Beginning Premium (5)	Ending Premium (6)=(5)-(3)	Ending Carrying Value (7)=(1)-(3)
7/1/X0 (A)	11,246						
12/31/X0	11,246	600	62	538	1,246	1,184	11,184
6/30/X1	11,184	600	62	538	1,184	1,122	11,122
12/31/X1	11,122	600	62	538	1,122	1,060	11,060
6/30/X2	11,060	600	62	538	1,060	998	10,998
12/31/X2	10,998	600	62	538	998	936	10,936
6/30/X3	10,936	600	62	538	936	874	10,874
12/31/X3	10,874	600	62	538	874	812	10,812
6/30/X4	10,812	600	62	538	812	750	10,750
12/31/X4	10,750	600	62	538	750	688	10,688
6/30/X5	10,688	600	62	538	688	626	10,626
12/31/X5	10,626	600	62	538	626	564	10,564

Date	Beginning Carrying Value (1)	Interest Payment (2)	Premium Amortized (3)	Total Interest Expense (4)=(2)-(3)	Beginning Premium (5)	Ending Premium (6)=(5)-(3)	Ending Carrying Value (7)=(1)-(3)
6/30/X6	10,564	600	62	538	564	502	10,502
12/31/X6	10,502	600	62	538	502	440	10,440
6/30/X7	10,440	600	62	538	440	378	10,378
12/31/X7	10,378	600	62	538	378	316	10,316
6/30/X8	10,316	600	62	538	316	254	10,254
12/31/X8	10,254	600	62	538	254	192	10,192
6/30/X9	10,192	600	62	538	192	130	10,130
12/31/X9	10,130	600	62	538	130	68	10,068
6/30/X10	10,068	600	* 68	532	68	0	10,000
		12,000	623	10,754			

* Due to rounding.

(A) At issue, carrying value = $10,000 face value + $1,246 premium.

The *effective interest method* of amortizing the premium calculates interest expense using the carrying value of the bonds and the market interest rate when the bonds were issued. For the first payment, the interest expense is $562. It is calculated by multiplying the $11,246 (carrying value of the bonds) times 10% (market interest rate) × 6/12 (semiannual payment). The amount of interest paid is $600 ($10,000 face value of bonds × 12% coupon interest rate × 6/12 semiannual payments). The $38 of premium amortization is the difference between the interest expense and the interest paid. The entry to record the first interest payment on December 31 using the effective interest method of amortizing the premium would be:

General Journal

Date	Account Title and Description	Ref.	Debit	Credit
Dec. 31	Interest Expense ($11,246 × 10% × 6/12)		562	
	Premium on Bonds Payable		38	
	Cash ($10,000 × 12% × 6/12)			600
	Pay semiannual interest using interest method of amortization			

As the premium is amortized, the balance in the premium account and the carrying value of the bond decreases. The amount of premium amortized for the last payment is equal to the balance in the premium on bonds payable account. As with the straight-line method of amortizing the premium, the effective interest method of amortizing the premium results in the premium account's balance being zero at the maturity of the bonds such that the carrying value of the bonds will be the same as the their principal amount. See Table 2-4 for interest expense and carrying value calculations over the life of the bonds using the effective interest method of amortizing the premium. At maturity, the General Journal entry to record the principal repayment is shown in the entry that follows Table 2-4.

Table 2-4: Effective Interest Method of Amortizing the Premium

Date	Beginning Carrying Value (1)	Interest Expense (2)	Premium Amortized (3)=(4)-(2)	Interest Payment (4)	Beginning Premium (5)	Ending Premium (6)=(5)-(3)	Ending Carrying Value (7)=(1)-(3)
7/1/X0 (A)	11,246						
12/31/X0	11,246	562	38	600	1,246	1,208	11,208
6/30/X1	11,208	560	40	600	1,208	1,168	11,168
12/31/X1	11,168	558	42	600	1,168	1,126	11,126
6/30/X2	11,126	556	44	600	1,126	1,082	11,082
12/31/X2	11,082	554	46	600	1,082	1,036	11,036
6/30/X3	11,036	552	48	600	1,036	988	10,988
12/31/X3	10,988	549	51	600	988	937	10,937
6/30/X4	10,937	547	53	600	937	884	10,884
12/31/X4	10,884	544	56	600	884	828	10,828
6/30/X5	10,828	541	59	600	828	769	10,769
12/31/X5	10,769	539	61	600	769	708	10,708
6/30/X6	10,708	535	65	600	708	643	10,643

Date	Beginning Carrying Value (1)	Interest Expense (2)	Premium Amortized (3)=(4)-(2)	Interest Payment (4)	Beginning Premium (5)	Ending Premium (6)=(5)-(3)	Ending Carrying Value (7)=(1)-(3)
12/31/X6	10,643	532	68	600	643	575	10,575
6/30/X7	10,575	529	71	600	575	504	10,504
12/31/X7	10,504	525	75	600	504	429	10,429
6/30/X8	10,429	521	79	600	429	350	10,350
12/31/X8	10,350	518	82	600	350	268	10,268
6/30/X9	10,268	513	87	600	268	181	10,181
12/31/X9	10,181	509	91	600	181	90	10,090
6/30/X10	10,090	* 510	* 90	600	90	0	10,000
		10,754	1,246	12,000			

* Due to rounding.

(A) At issue, carrying value = $10,000 face value + $1,246 premium.

General Journal

Date	Account Title and Description	Ref.	Debit	Credit
July 1	Bonds Payable		10,000	
	Cash			10,000
	Repay bond principal at maturity			

Bonds issued between interest dates

If a bond is sold at a time other than on its original issue date, the purchaser of the bond pays the issuing company the price of the bond plus accrued interest from the last interest payment date. This accrued interest is paid back to the purchaser who receives six months of interest at the next semiannual interest payment date. For example, if Lighting Process, Inc. issued $10,000 ten-year 10% bonds dated July 1, 20X0, on September 1, 20X0, the purchaser would pay the $10,000 for the bonds and interest of $167 ($10,000 × 10% × $\frac{2}{12}$) for two months. On December 31, the purchaser would receive a semiannual interest payment of $500 ($10,000 × 10% × $\frac{6}{12}$) as if the purchaser had owned the bonds for the entire six-month period. The entries for these two events would be:

General Journal

Date	Account Title and Description	Ref.	Debit	Credit
20X0				
Sept. 1	Cash		10,167	
	Bonds Payable			10,000
	Bond Interest Payable ($10,000 × 10% × $\frac{2}{12}$)			167

Date	Account Title and Description	Ref.	Debit	Credit
	Issue $10,000 10% bonds dated 7/1			
Dec. 31	Bond Interest Payable		167	
	Bond Interest Expense ($10,000 × 10% × $^4\!/_{12}$)		333	
	Cash			500
	Pay semiannual interest			

Deferred Income Taxes

Many companies report different amounts of income on their income statement and on their income tax return. This difference occurs because the definition of income is not the same under GAAP (generally accepted accounting principles) and federal income tax regulations. GAAP requires income tax expense to be calculated on income before taxes on the income statement while the tax return calculates taxes due based on taxable income per the income tax return.

If the differences are considered temporary, in other words, if certain revenues and/or expenses are reported in different years in income statements and on income tax returns, an asset or liability called deferred income tax exists. If deferred income tax represents the portion of the income tax expense that will be *paid* in future years, a long-term liability called deferred taxes is recorded on the balance sheet.

A **partnership** is an unincorporated association of two or more individuals to carry on a business for profit. Many small businesses, including retail, service, and professional practitioners, are organized as partnerships.

Characteristics of a Partnership

A partnership agreement may be oral or written. However, to avoid misunderstandings, the partnership agreement should be in writing. The agreement should identify the partners; their respective business-related duties and responsibilities; how income will be shared; the criteria for additional investments and withdrawals; and the guidelines for adding partners, the withdrawal of a partner, and liquidation of the partnership. For income tax purposes, the partnership files an information return only. Each partner shares in the net income or loss of the partnership and includes this amount on his/her own tax return.

Limited life
The life of a partnership may be established as a certain number of years by the agreement. If no such agreement is made, the death, inability to carry out specific responsibilities, bankruptcy, or the desire of a partner to withdraw automatically terminates the partnership. Every time a partner withdraws or is added, a new partnership agreement is required if the business will continue to operate as a partnership. With proper provisions, the partnership's business may continue and the termination or withdrawal of the partnership will be a documentation issue that does not impact ongoing operations of the partnership.

Mutual agency

In a partnership, the partners are agents for the partnership. As such, one partner may legally bind the partnership to a contract or agreement that appears to be in line with the partnership's operations. As most partnerships create unlimited liability for its partners, it is important to know something about potential partners before beginning a partnership. Although partners may limit a partner's ability to enter into contracts on the company's behalf, this limit only applies if the third party entering into the contract is aware of the limitation. It is the partners' responsibility to notify third parties that a particular partner is limited in his or her ability to enter into contracts.

Unlimited liability

Partners may be called on to use their personal assets to satisfy partnership debts when the partnership cannot meet its obligations. If one partner does not have sufficient assets to meet his/her share of the partnership's debt, the other partners can be held individually liable by the creditor requiring payment. A partnership in which all partners are individually liable is called a **general partnership**. A **limited partnership** has two classes of partners and is often used when investors will not be actively involved in the business and do not want to risk their personal assets. A limited partnership must include at least one general partner who maintains unlimited liability. The liability of other partners is limited to the amount of their investments. Therefore, they are called limited partners. A limited partnership usually has LLP in its name.

Ease of formation

Other than registration of the business, a partnership has few requirements to be formed.

Transfer of ownership

Although it is relatively easy to dissolve a partnership, the transfer of ownership, whether to a new or existing partner, requires approval of the remaining partners.

Management structure and operations

In most partnerships, the partners are involved in operating the business. Their regular involvement makes critical decisions easier as formal meetings are not required to get approval before action can be taken. If the partners agree on a change in strategy or structure, or approve a purchase of needed equipment, no additional approvals are needed.

Relative lack of regulation

Most governmental regulations and reporting requirements are written for corporations. Although the number of sole proprietors and partnerships exceeds the number of corporations, the level of sales and profits generated by corporations are much greater.

Number of partners

The informality of decision making in a partnership tends to work well with a small number of partners. Having a large number of partners, particularly if all are involved in operating the business, can make decisions much more difficult.

Partnership Accounting

Except for the number of partners' equity accounts, accounting for a partnership is the same as accounting for a sole proprietor. Each partner has a separate capital account for investments and his/her share of net income or loss, and a separate withdrawal account. A **withdrawal account** is used to track the amount taken from the business for personal use. The net income or loss is added to the capital accounts in the closing process. The withdrawal account is also closed to the capital account in the closing process.

Asset contributions to partnerships

When a partnership is formed or a partner is added and contributes assets other than cash, the partnership establishes the net realizable or fair market value for the assets. For example, if the Walking Partners company adds a partner who contributes accounts receivable and equipment from an existing business, the partnership evaluates the collectibility of the accounts receivable and records them at their net realizable value. An existing valuation reserve account (usually called allowance for doubtful accounts) would not be transferred to the partnership as the partnership would establish its own reserve account. Similarly, any existing accumulated depreciation accounts are not assumed by the partnership. The partnership establishes and records the equipment at its current fair market value and then begins depreciating the equipment over its useful life to the partnership.

Income allocations

The partnership agreement should include how the net income or loss will be allocated to the partners. If the agreement is silent, the net income or loss is allocated equally to all partners. As partners are the owners of the business, they do not receive a salary but each has the right to withdraw assets up to the level of his/her capital account balance. Some partnership agreements refer to salaries or salary allowances for partners and interest on investments. These are not expenses of the business, they are part of the formula for splitting net income. Many partners use the components of the formula for splitting net income or loss to determine how much they will withdraw in cash from the business during the year, in anticipation of their share of net income. If the partnership uses the accrual basis of accounting, the partners pay federal income taxes on their share of net income, regardless of how much cash they actually withdraw from the partnership during the year.

Once net income is allocated to the partners, it is transferred to the individual partners' capital accounts through closing entries. For example, assume Dee's Consultants, Inc., a partnership, earned $60,000 and their agreement is that all profits are shared equally. Each of the three partners would be allocated $20,000 ($60,000 ÷ 3). The journal entry to record this allocation of net income would be:

General Journal

Date	Account Title and Description	Ref.	Debit	Credit
20X0				
Dec.31	Income Summary		60,000	
	Dee, Capital			20,000
	Sue, Capital			20,000
	Jeanette, Capital			20,000
	Transfer net income to partners' capital accounts			

Remember that allocating net income does not mean the partners receive cash. Cash is paid to a partner only when it is withdrawn from the partnership.

In addition to sharing equally, net income may also be split according to agreed upon percentages (for example, 50%, 40%, and 10%), ratios (2:3:1), or fractions ($\frac{1}{3}$, $\frac{1}{3}$, and $\frac{1}{3}$). Using Dee's Consultants net income of $60,000 and a partnership agreement that says net income is shared 50%, 40%, and 10% by its partners, the portion of net income allocated to each partner is simply the $60,000 multiplied by the individual partner's ownership percentage. Using this information, the split of net income would be:

Dee	50%	$30,000
Sue	40%	24,000
Jeanette	10%	6,000
Total net income		$60,000

Using the 2:3:1 ratio, first add the numbers together to find the total shares (six in this case) and then multiply the net income by a fraction of the individual partner's share to the total parts (2/6, 3/6, and 1/6). Using the three ratios, the $60,000 of Dee's Consultants net income would be split as follows:

Sue	2/6	20,000
Dee	3/6	$30,000
Jeanette	1/6	10,000
Total net income		$60,000

Using the fractions of 1/3, 1/3, and 1/3, the net income would be split equally to all three partners, and each partner's capital account balance would increase by $20,000.

Assume the partnership agreement for Dee's Consultants requires net income to be allocated based on three criteria, including: salary allowances of $15,000, $12,000, and $5,000 for Dee, Sue, and Jeanette, respectively; 10% interest on each partner's beginning capital balance; and any remainder to be split equally. Using this information, the $60,000 of net income would be allocated $21,000 to Dee, $20,000 to Sue, and $19,000 to Jeanette.

Information from the owners' capital accounts shows the following activity:

	Beginning Capital Balance	Additional Investments During Year	Withdrawals During Year
Dee	$ 20,000	$ 5,000	$15,000
Sue	40,000	5,000	10,000
Jeanette	100,000	10,000	5,000

Allocation of Net Income of $60,000

	Dee	Sue	Jeanette	Total
Salary Allowances	$15,000	$12,000	$ 5,000	$32,000
Interest (10% of beginning capital account balance)	2,000	4,000	10,000	16,000
	17,000	16,000	15,000	48,000
Remainder (equally)	4,000	4,000	4,000	12,000
Net Income	$21,000	$20,000	$19,000	$60,000

The investments and withdrawal activity did not impact the calculation of net income because they are not part of the agreed method to allocate net income. As can be seen, once the salary and interest portions are determined, they are added together to determine the amount of the remainder to be allocated. The remainder may be a positive or negative amount.

Assume the same facts as above except change net income to $39,000. After allocating the salary allowances of $32,000 and interest of $16,000, too much net income has been allocated. The difference between the $48,000 allocated and the $39,000 net income, a decrease of $9,000, is the remainder to be allocated equally to each partner. These assumptions would result in allocations of net income to Dee of $14,000, Sue of $13,000, and Jeanette of $12,000. The calculations are as shown:

Allocation of Net Income of $39,000

	Dee	Sue	Jeanette	Total
Salary allowances	$15,000	$12,000	$ 5,000	$32,000
Interest (10% of beginning capital account balance)	2,000	4,000	10,000	16,000
	17,000	16,000	15,000	48,000
Remainder (equally)	(3,000)	(3,000)	(3,000)	(9,000)
Net Income	$14,000	$13,000	$12,000	$39,000

Changes in Partners

Partnerships can change with the addition or withdrawal of partners. This section discusses how to account for those changes.

New partner

Partners may agree to add partners in one or two ways. First, the new partner could buy out all or a portion of the interest of an existing partner or partners. Second, the new partner could invest in the partnership resulting in an increase in the number of partners. The partnership accounts for these changes in partners differently.

Buying out existing partner. The capital balances of an existing partnership are:

MJM	$ 70,000
EAM	50,000
Total partnership capital	$120,000

If MJM decides to retire and the partners agree to have TLM buy out MJM's partnership interest, the partnership's accounting records must simply reflect the change of ownership. As TLM is buying out MJM's entire interest directly from MJM, the partnership's entry to record the transaction is as follows:

General Journal

Date	Account Title and Description	Ref.	Debit	Credit
20X0				
Mar. 10	MJM, Capital		70,000	
	TLM, Capital			70,000
	Buyout of MJM by TLM			

The cash that MJM receives from TLM is not recorded on the partnership's books as it is an exchange of an investment by individuals with no assets being given to or taken from the partnership. Therefore, it does not matter whether TLM pays $50,000, $70,000, or $100,000 for MJM's partnership interest, the partnership simply records the change in the partner's capital accounts using the current balance in the MJM, capital account.

Investment in the partnership. If TLM joins the existing partnership (becoming a third partner) by investing cash of $30,000 in the partnership, the partnership must record the additional cash and establish a capital account for the new partner. The amount recorded as capital for TLM depends on his ownership interest in the partnership. If a difference exists between the cash TLM contributes to the partnership and his ownership interest, the difference is allocated to the existing partners. This difference may increase the existing partners' capital account balances (a bonus to existing partners) or be deducted from the existing partners' capital account balances (a bonus to the new partner).

If TLM receives a 20% ownership interest in the partnership for his $30,000 investment, the amount of his initial capital account balance is calculated by adding the $30,000 to the total partnership's capital before his investment and multiplying by 20%, TLM's ownership interest. TLM's capital account would be credited for $30,000 in this case.

Existing Capital	
MJM, Capital	$ 70,000
EAM, Capital	50,000
Total Existing Capital	120,000
Add: TLM Investment	30,000
New Capital Balance	150,000
TLM Ownership %	× 20%
TLM, Capital	$ 30,000

The entry to record TLM's investment into the partnership would be:

General Journal

Date	Account Title and Description	Ref.	Debit	Credit
20X0				
Mar. 10	Cash		30,000	
	TLM, Capital			30,000
	Investment in partnership by TLM			

If TLM receives a 30% interest for his $30,000 investment, TLM's capital account would be credited for $45,000.

Existing Capital	
MJM, Capital	$ 70,000
EAM, Capital	50,000
Total Existing Capital	120,000
Add: TLM Investment	30,000
New Capital Balance	150,000
TLM Ownership %	× 30%
TLM, Capital	$ 45,000

The $15,000 difference between his initial capital balance of $45,000 and his cash investment of $30,000 must be deducted from the existing partners' capital account balances according to their sharing of gains and losses. If the current ratio for sharing gains and losses is 60%:40%, the partnership would record TLM's 30% interest with the following entry:

General Journal

Date	Account Title and Description	Ref.	Debit	Credit
20X0				
Mar. 10	Cash		30,000	
	MJM, Capital ($15,000 × 60%)		9,000	
	EAM, Capital ($15,000 × 40%)		6,000	
	TLM, Capital			45,000
	Investment in partnership by TLM			

If TLM receives a 15% interest in the partnership for his $30,000 investment, the partnership's cash account would be increased (debited) by $30,000 and TLM's capital account would be increased (credited) by $22,500 (15% × $150,000 new capital balance of partnership).

Existing Capital	
MJM, Capital	$ 70,000
EAM, Capital	50,000
Total Existing Capital	120,000
Add: TLM Investment	30,000
New Capital Balance	150,000
TLM Ownership %	× 15%
TLM, Capital	$ 22,500

The remaining $7,500 would be added (credited) to the two existing partners' capital account balances based on their 60%:40% ratio for sharing gains and losses. MJM's capital account balance would increase $4,500 and EAM's capital account balance would increase $3,000. The entry would look like:

General Journal

Date	Account Title and Description	Ref.	Debit	Credit
20X0				
Mar. 10	Cash		30,000	
	MJM, Capital ($7,500 × 60%)			4,500
	EAM, Capital ($7,500 × 40%)			3,000
	TLM, Capital			22,500
	Investment in partnership by TLM			

Retirement or withdrawal of a partner

If an existing partner wishes to retire or withdraw from the partnership, the partner may be bought out by an existing partner or may receive assets from the partnership. The accounting treatment for retirements is similar to that discussed under the section "New Partner." If an existing partner purchases the interest of the retiring partner, the partnership records an entry to close out the capital account balance of the retiring partner and adds the amount to the capital account balance of the partner who purchased the interest. If the partnership gives assets to the retiring partner in the amount of the partner's capital account balance, an entry is made to reduce the assets and zero out the retiring partner's capital account balance. If the retiring partner receives more assets or fewer assets than the partner's capital account balance, the difference is taken from or added to the capital accounts of the remaining partners according to how they share in gains or losses.

Liquidation of a Partnership

If the partnership decides to liquidate, the assets of the partnership are sold, liabilities are paid off, and any remaining cash is distributed to the partners according to their capital account balances. If a partner's capital account has a deficit balance, that partner should contribute the amount of the deficit to the partnership.

The Statement of Partners' Capital

The statement of partners' capital shows the changes in each partner's capital account for the year or period being reported on. It has the same format as the statement of owner's equity except that it includes a column for each partner and a total column for the company rather than just one column. The statement starts with the beginning capital balance, followed by the amounts of investments made, share of net income or loss, and withdrawals made during the reporting period to determine the capital balance at the end of the period.

The Midland Connection
Statement of Partners' Capital
For the Year ended December 31, 20X0

	Minbiole, CPA	Kaschalk, CPA	Total Partnership
Capital balances, January 1, 20X0	$ 50,000	$ 100,000	$ 150,000
Add: Investments	25,000	10,000	35,000
Net Income	40,000	40,000	80,000
Less: Withdrawals	(45,000)	(30,000)	(75,000)
Capital balances, December 31, 20X0	$ 70,000	$ 120,000	$ 190,000

The $190,000 capital balance for the partnership at December 31, 20X0 would be the amount reported as owners' equity in The Midland Connection's balance sheet as of December 31, 20X0.

A **corporation** is a legal entity, meaning it is a separate entity from its owners who are called stockholders. A corporation is treated as a "person" with most of the rights and obligations of a real person. A corporation is not allowed to hold public office or vote, but it does pay income taxes. It may be established as a profit making or non-profit organization and may be publicly or privately held. The stock of a public company is traded on a stock exchange. There may be thousands, even millions, of stockholders in a public company. Stock of a privately held company is not traded on an exchange and there are usually only a small number of stockholders.

To be recognized as a corporation, a business must file an application that includes the corporation's articles of incorporation (charter) with the State, pay an incorporation fee, and be approved by the State. Once the approval is received, the corporation must develop its bylaws. **Organization costs**, including legal fees, underwriters' fees for stock and bond issues, and incorporation fees, are recorded as an intangible asset and amortized over a period of time not to exceed 40 years.

Ownership in a corporation is represented by **stock certificates**, which is why the owners are called **stockholders**. Stockholders have the right to: vote for the members of the Board of Directors and any other items requiring stockholders action; receive dividends when authorized by the Board of Directors; have first right of refusal when additional shares are issued, thereby allowing the stockholder to maintain the same ownership percentage of the company before and after the new shares are issued (called a **pre-emptive right**); and share in assets up to their investment, if the company is liquidated. In some states, stockholders are called **shareholders**.

Characteristics of a Corporation

A number of characteristics distinguish a corporation from a sole proprietor or partnership.

Unlimited life

As a corporation is owned by stockholders and managed by employees, the sale of stock, death of a stockholder, or inability of an employee to function does not impact the continuous life of the corporation. Its charter may limit the corporation's life although the corporation may continue if the charter is extended.

Limited liability

The liability of stockholders is limited to the amount each has invested in the corporation. Personal assets of stockholders are not available to creditors or lenders seeking payment of amounts owed by the corporation. Creditors are limited to corporate assets for satisfaction of their claims.

Separate legal entity

The corporation is considered a separate legal entity, conducting business in its own name. Therefore, corporations may own property, enter into binding contracts, borrow money, sue and be sued, and pay taxes. Stockholders are agents for the corporation only if they are also employees or designated as agents.

Relative ease of transferring ownership rights

A person who buys stock in a corporation is called a stockholder and receives a stock certificate indicating the number of shares of the company she/he has purchased. Particularly in a public company, the stock can be easily transferred in part or total at the discretion of the stockholder. The stockholder wishing to transfer (sell) stock does not require the approval of the other stockholders to sell the stock. Similarly, a person or an entity wishing to purchase stock in a corporation does not require the approval of the corporation or its existing stockholders before purchasing the stock. Once a public corporation sells its initial offering of stock, it is not part of any subsequent transfers except as a record keeper of share ownership. Privately held companies may have some restrictions on the transfer of stock.

Professional management
Investors in a corporation need not actively manage the business, as most corporations hire professional managers to operate the business. The investors vote on the Board of Directors who are responsible for hiring management.

Ease of capital acquisition
A corporation can obtain capital by selling stock or bonds. This gives a corporation a larger pool of resources because it is not limited to the resources of a small number of individuals. The limited liability and ease of transferring ownership rights makes it easier for a corporation to acquire capital by selling stock, and the size of the corporation allows it to issue bonds based on its name.

Government regulations
The sale of stock results in government regulation to protect stockholders, the owners of the corporation. State laws usually include the requirements for issuing stock and distributions to stockholders. The federal securities laws also govern the sale of stock. Publicly held companies with stock traded on exchanges are required to file their financial statements and additional informative disclosures with the Securities and Exchange Commission. Certain industries, such as banks, financial institutions, and gaming, are also subject to regulations from other governmental agencies.

Stock Terminology

Before discussing the accounting for stock, it may be helpful to understand the following stock terms.

- **Authorized stock.** Per the articles of incorporation, the type and number of shares of stock a corporation may sell. Approval by stockholders is required to issue any shares above the authorized level.

- **Issued stock.** The number of shares transferred to stockholders in exchange for cash, assets, or services rendered.

- **Outstanding stock.** Issued stock that is held by stockholders and has not been bought back by the corporation.

- **Treasury stock.** Issued stock that has been bought back by the corporation.

- **Market value.** The price set by interested buyers and sellers for the stock of publicly traded companies.

- **Par value.** The value assigned in a corporation's articles of incorporation to one share of stock. It appears on the stock certificate. In some states, the par value of all outstanding shares is considered the legal capital of a corporation. **Legal capital** is the amount of contributed capital that must remain in the corporation and may not be paid out in dividends.

- **Contributed capital.** Also called paid-in capital, it is the amount of value received by the corporation when it issues its stock. It includes the par value and any amount received in excess of the par value.

- **No-par value stock.** Shares of stock that do not include a par value. The Board of Directors may assign a value to this type of stock.

- **Stated value.** The value assigned to no-par value stock by the Board of Directors of a corporation.

- **Common stock.** The class of stock issued most frequently by a corporation. Common stock ownership normally includes the rights to vote on stockholder matters, to receive dividends only after preferred stockholders, and, in the event of a liquidation, to receive their investment back if anything remained after the creditors were paid and the investment of the preferred stockholders was returned to them. It may have a par value or be no-par value stock that may or may not have a stated value.

- **Preferred stock.** Preferred stock is a class of stock that normally has the right to receive dividends, and in the case of liquidation of the corporation, a return of investment before the common stockholders. Preferred stock usually does not include a voting right.

- **Dividends.** A dividend is a distribution by a corporation to its owners in the form of cash, assets, or the company's stock. Stockholders do not have withdrawal accounts like sole proprietors or partners because the only way they can get money from the corporation is if the Board of Directors authorizes a dividend.

- **Stockholders' equity.** In a corporation's balance sheet, the owners' equity section is called **stockholders' equity**. It includes the contributed capital accounts and retained earnings.

- **Retained earnings.** The amount of net income a corporation has earned since it began in business that has not been distributed as dividends to its stockholders. Net income increases retained earnings. Dividends, net losses, and some treasury stock transactions decrease retained earnings. Net income, and dividends, if they are recorded in a separate account, are transferred to retained earnings during the closing entry process.

Accounting for Stock Transactions

This section demonstrates how to account for stock transactions.

Stock issued for cash

Corporations may issue stock for cash.

Common stock. When a company such as Big City Dwellers issues 5,000 shares of its $1 par value common stock at par for cash, that means the company will receive $5,000 (5,000 shares × $1 per share). The sale of the stock is recorded by increasing (debiting) cash and increasing (crediting) common stock by $5,000.

General Journal

Date	Account Title and Description	Ref.	Debit	Credit
20X0				
June 1	Cash		5,000	
	Common Stock			5,000
	Sale of stock			

If the Big City Dwellers sold their $1 par value stock for $5 per share, they would receive $25,000 (5,000 shares × $5 per share) and would record the difference between the $5,000 par value of the stock (5,000 shares × $1 par value per share) and the cash received as additional paid-in-capital in excess of par value (often called additional paid-in-capital).

General Journal

Date	Account Title and Description	Ref.	Debit	Credit
20X0				
June 1	Cash		25,000	
	Common Stock (5,000 × $1)			5,000
	Additional Paid-in-Capital			20,000
	Sale of 5,000 shares of stock at $5 per share			

When no-par value stock is issued and the Board of Directors establishes a stated value for legal purposes, the stated value is treated like the par value when recording the stock transaction. If the Board of Directors has not specified a stated value, the entire amount received when the shares are sold is recorded in the common stock account. If a corporation has both par value and no-par value common stock, separate common stock accounts must be maintained.

Preferred stock. The sale of preferred stock is accounted for using these same principles. A separate set of accounts should be used for the par value of preferred stock and any additional paid-in-capital in excess of par value for preferred stock. Preferred stock may have a **call price**, which is the amount the "issuing" company could pay to buy back the preferred stock at a specified future date. If Big City Dwellers issued 1,000 shares of its $1 par value preferred stock for $100 per share, the entry to record the sale would increase (debit) cash by $100,000 (1,000 shares × $100 per share), increase (credit) preferred stock by the par value, or $1,000 (1,000 shares × $1 par value), and increase (credit) additional paid-in-capital—preferred stock for the difference of $99,000.

General Journal

Date	Account Title and Description	Ref.	Debit	Credit
20X0				
June 1	Cash		100,000	
	Preferred Stock (1,000 × $1)			1,000
	Additional Paid-in-Capital (Preferred Stock)			99,000
	Sale of 1,000 shares of preferred stock at $100 per share			

Stock issued in exchange for assets or services

If corporations issue stock in exchange for assets or as payment for services rendered, a value must be assigned using the cost principle. The cost of an asset received in exchange for a corporation's stock is the market value of the stock issued. If the stock's market value is not yet determined (as would occur when a company is just starting), the fair market value of the assets or services received is used to value the transaction. If the total value exceeds the par or stated value of the stock issued, the value in excess of the par or stated value is added to the additional paid-in-capital (or paid-in-capital in excess of par) account. For example, The J Trio, Inc., *a start-up company*, issues 10,000 shares of its $0.50 par value common stock to its attorney in payment of a $50,000 invoice from the attorney for costs incurred by the law firm to help establish the corporation. The entry to record this exchange would be based on the invoice value because the market value for the corporation's stock has not yet been determined. The entry to record the transaction increases (debits) organization costs for $50,000, increases (credits) common stock for $5,000 (10,000 shares × $0.50 par value), and increases (credits) additional paid-in-capital for $45,000 (the difference). Organization costs is an intangible asset, included on the balance sheet and amortized over some period not to exceed 40 years.

General Journal

Date	Account Title and Description	Ref.	Debit	Credit
20X0				
July 1	Organization Costs		50,000	
	Common Stock (10,000 × $0.50)			5,000
	Additional Paid-in-Capital			45,000
	Issue 10,000 shares to settle attorney's invoice for start-up costs			

If The J Trio, Inc., *an established corporation*, issues 10,000 shares of its $1 par value common stock in exchange for land to be used as a plant site, the market value of the stock on the date it is issued is used to value the transaction. The fair market value of the land cannot be objectively determined as it relies on an individual's opinion and therefore, the more objective stock price is used in valuing the land.

The stock transactions discussed here all relate to the initial sale or issuance of stock by The J Trio, Inc. Subsequent transactions between stockholders are not accounted for by The J Trio, Inc. and have no effect on the value of stockholders' equity on the balance sheet. Stockholders' equity is affected only if the corporation issues additional stock or buys back its own stock.

Treasury stock

Treasury stock is the corporation's issued stock that has been bought back from the stockholders. As a corporation cannot be its own shareholder, any shares purchased by the corporation are not considered assets of the corporation. Assuming the corporation plans to re-issue the shares in the future, the shares are held in treasury and reported as a reduction in stockholders' equity in the balance sheet. Shares of treasury stock do not have the right to vote, receive dividends, or receive a liquidation value. Companies purchase treasury stock if shares are needed for employee compensation plans or to acquire another company, and to reduce the number of outstanding shares because the stock is considered a good buy. Purchasing treasury stock may stimulate trading, and without changing net income, will increase earnings per share.

The **cost method** of accounting for treasury stock records the amount paid to repurchase stock as an increase (debit) to treasury stock and a decrease (credit) to cash. The treasury stock account is a contra account to the other stockholders' equity accounts and therefore, has a debit balance. No distinction is made between the par or stated value of the stock and the premium paid by the company. To illustrate, assume The Soccer Trio Corporation repurchases 15,000 shares of its $1 par value common stock for $25 per share. To record this transaction, treasury stock is increased (debited) by $375,000 (15,000 shares × $25 per share) and cash is decreased (credited) by a corresponding amount. The entry looks like the following:

General Journal

Date	Account Title and Description	Ref.	Debit	Credit
20X0				
Dec.3	Treasury Stock		375,000	
	Cash			375,000
	Repurchase 15,000 shares at $25			

In the balance sheet, treasury stock is reported as a contra account after retained earnings in the stockholders' equity section. This means the amount reported as treasury stock is subtracted from the other stockholders' equity amounts. Treasury shares are included in the number reported for shares issued but are subtracted from issued shares to determine the number of outstanding shares.

When treasury stock is sold, the accounts used to record the sale depend on whether the treasury stock was sold above or below the cost paid to purchase it. If the treasury stock is sold above its cost, the sale increases (debits) cash for the proceeds received, decreases (credits) treasury stock for the cost paid when the treasury stock was repurchased, and increases (credits) additional paid-in-capital—treasury stock for the difference between the selling price and the repurchase price. If Soccer Trio Corporation subsequently sells 7,500 of the shares repurchased for $25 for $28, the entry to record the sale would be as shown:

General Journal

Date	Account Title and Description	Ref.	Debit	Credit
20X1				
June 15	Cash (7,500 × $28)		210,000	
	Treasury Stock (7,500 × $25)			187,500
	Additional paid-in-capital (treasury stock)			22,500
	Record sale of 7,500 shares of treasury stock at $28			

When the remaining 7,500 shares are sold, the entry to record the sale includes an increase (debit) to cash for the proceeds received, a decrease (credit) to treasury stock for the repurchase price of $25 per

share or $187,500, and a decrease (debit) to additional paid-in-capital
× treasury stock, if the account has a balance, for the difference. If
the difference between cash received and the cost of the treasury
stock is greater than the additional paid-in-capital—treasury stock
account, retained earnings is reduced (debited) for the remaining
amount after the additional paid-in-capita—treasury stock account
balance is reduced to zero. If Soccer Trio Corporation sells the
remaining 7,500 shares of its treasury stock for $21, the entry to
record the sale would be as shown:

General Journal

Date	Account Title and Description	Ref.	Debit	Credit
20X1				
June 25	Cash (7,500 × $21)		157,500	
	Additional paid-in-capital (treasury stock)		22,500	
	Retained Earnings		7,500	
	Treasury Stock (7,500 × $25)			187,500
	Record sale of 7,500 shares of treasury stock at $21			

If the Board of Directors decides to **retire the treasury stock** at
the time it is repurchased, it is cancelled and no longer considered
issued. When this occurs, the common stock and additional paid-in-
capital accounts are decreased (debited) for the amounts recorded in
these accounts when the stock was originally issued and cash is
decreased (credited) for the amount paid to repurchase the stock. If
the repurchase price is more than the original issue price, the difference is a decrease (debit) to the additional paid-in-capital—treasury
stock account until its balance reaches zero. Once the balance in the
additional paid-in-capital—treasury stock account reaches zero, or if

there is no such account, the difference is a decrease (debit) to retained earnings. If the repurchase price is less than the original selling price, the difference increases (is credited to) the additional paid-in-capital account.

Dividends

The Board of Directors must authorize all dividends. A dividend may distribute cash, assets, or the corporation's own stock to its stockholders. Distribution of assets, also called property dividends, will not be discussed here. Before authorizing a dividend, a company must have sufficient retained earnings and cash (cash dividend) or sufficient authorized stock (stock dividend). Three dates are relevant when accounting for dividends:

- Date of declaration.
- Date of record.
- Date of payment or distribution.

The **date of declaration** is the date the Board of Directors formally authorizes for the payment of a cash dividend or issuance of shares of stock. This date establishes the liability of the company. On this date, the value of the dividend to be paid or distributed is deducted from retained earnings. The **date of record** does not require a formal accounting entry. It establishes who will receive the dividend. The **date of payment or distribution** is when the dividend is given to the stockholders of record.

If a company has both preferred and common stockholders, the preferred stockholders receive a preference if any dividend is declared. Having the preference does not guarantee preferred stockholders a dividend, it just puts them first in line if a dividend is paid. Preferred stock usually specifies a dividend percentage or a flat dollar amount. For example, preferred stock with a $100 par value has a 5%

or $5 dividend rate. Five percent is the $5 dividend divided by the $100 par value. This means all preferred stockholders will receive a $5 per share dividend *before* any dividend is paid to common stockholders. Some shares of preferred stock have special dividend features such as cumulative dividend or participating dividend.

A cumulative dividend means if dividends are declared, preferred stockholders will receive their current-year dividend plus any dividends not paid in prior years before the common stockholders receive a dividend. Owning a share of preferred stock that includes a cumulative dividend still does not guarantee the preferred stockholder a dividend because the company is not liable to pay dividends until they are declared. Having cumulative preferred stock simply reinforces the preference preferred stockholders receive when a dividend is declared. If a company has issued cumulative preferred stock and does not declare a dividend, the company has **dividends in arrears**. Although not a liability, the amount of any dividends in arrears must be disclosed in the financial statements.

The **participating dividend** feature provides the opportunity for the preferred stockholders to receive dividends above the stated rate. It occurs only after the common stockholders have received the same rate of return on their shares as the preferred stockholders. For example, say the preferred dividend rate is 5% and the preferred stock has a participating feature. This means that the preferred stockholders will receive a larger dividend if the authorized dividend exceeds the total of the 5% dividend for the preferred stockholder and a 5% dividend to the common stockholders.

Cash dividends

On May 1, the Board of Directors of Triple Play authorized payment of a $50,000 cash dividend on June 30 to the stockholders of record on May 25. On May 1, the **date of declaration**, the value of the dividend to be paid is deducted from (debited to) retained earnings and set up as a liability in a separate dividends payable account.

General Journal

Date	Account Title and Description	Ref.	Debit	Credit
20X1				
May 1	Retained Earnings		50,000	
	Dividend Payable			50,000
	Authorized dividend			

It should be noted that some companies use separate accounts called "Dividends, Common Stock" and "Dividends, Preferred Stock" rather than retained earnings to record dividends declared. If these accounts are used, a closing entry is made at the end of the period to decrease (debit) retained earnings and decrease (credit) "Dividends, Common Stock" and "Dividends, Preferred Stock" to zero out the balances in the dividend accounts and update the retained earnings balance.

On the **date of payment** when the cash is sent out to the stockholders, the dividends payable account is decreased (debited) and the cash account is decreased (credited).

General Journal

Date	Account Title and Description	Ref.	Debit	Credit
20X1				
June 30	Dividend Payable		50,000	
	Cash			50,000
	Pay dividend			

Once declared and paid, a cash dividend decreases total stockholders' equity and decreases total assets. Dividends are not reported on the income statement. They would be found in a statement of retained earnings or statement of stockholders' equity once declared and in a statement of cash flows when paid.

Stock dividends

Stock dividends are used when a company needs to maintain its cash in the business but wants to provide a dividend to its stockholders. The size of a stock dividend determines how it is valued. A small size dividend (less than 20—25% of outstanding shares) is usually valued at the market value of the stock. A large size dividend (more than 20—25% of outstanding shares) is usually valued at par or stated value.

Assume the Board of Directors of Grandma's Girls authorizes a 10% stock dividend on May 20th, distributable on July 17th to stockholders of record on June 9th when the stock is selling for $20 per share. Before the dividend, the company's balance sheet had the following stockholders' equity section:

Common Stock, $3 par value, 1,500,000 shares authorized, 500,000 shares issued and outstanding	$1,500,000
Additional Paid-in-Capital	6,000,000
Retained Earnings	2,325,000
Total stockholders' equity	$9,825,000

The $1,000,000 value of the dividend is determined by multiplying the 50,000 shares to be issued (10% × 500,000 outstanding shares) by $20 (market value of stock). The entry to record the declaration of the dividend decreases (debits) retained earnings for the $1,000,000 market value of the shares to be issued, increases (credits) common stock dividend distributable for the $150,000 par value of the shares to be issued ($3 × 50,000), and increases (credits) additional paid-in-capital for the difference between the par (or stated value) and the market value of $850,000 ($50,000 × ($20 − $3)).

General Journal

Date	Account Title and Description	Ref.	Debit	Credit
20X0				
May 20	Retained Earnings ((10% × 500,000 shares) × $20)		1,000,000	
	Common Stock Dividend Distributable (50,000 shares to be issued × $3 par)			150,000
	Additional Paid-in-Capital			850,000
	Authorize 10% stock dividend			

On July 17th when the shares of stock are distributed to the stock-holders, an entry is made to decrease (debit) common stock dividend distributable and increase (credit) common stock for $150,000, the par (or stated value).

General Journal

Date	Account Title and Description	Ref.	Debit	Credit
20X0				
July 17	Common Stock Dividend Distributable		150,000	
	Common Stock			150,000
	Issue shares for stock dividend			

The net effect of the entries recorded when a stock dividend is declared and distributed is a change in the components of stockholders' equity but not in total stockholders' equity or assets (see following page for example).

Stock Splits

A **stock split** occurs when a Board of Directors authorizes a change in the par or stated value of its stock. This reduction in par value is made to lower the market price of the stock to make the stock more attractive to potential investors. When a company's stock splits, the change in the par value is offset by a corresponding change in the number of shares so the total par value remains the same. The total stockholders' equity is unaffected by the stock split and no entries are recorded. For example, if Grandma's Girls declared a 3-for-1 stock split instead of a 10% stock dividend, the company would issue three shares in place of every one share currently held. After the split occurs, the par value or stated value is divided by 3 (because it is a 3-for-1 stock split) to determine the new par or stated value, and the number of outstanding shares is multiplied by 3. After the stock split, the new par value is $1 ($3 ÷ 3) and the number of outstanding shares is 1,500,000 (500,000 × 3). The total par value of the common stock remains at $1,500,000 (1,500,000 shares × $1 par value). The following chart illustrates the effects of stock dividends and stock splits on stockholders' equity.

Effect of Stock Dividends and
Stock Splits on Stockholders' Equity

	Before	After Stock Dividend	After Stock Split
Common Stock, $3 par	$1,500,000	$1,650,000	$1,500,000
Additional Paid-in-Capital	6,000,000	6,850,000	6,000,000
Retained Earnings	2,325,000	1,325,000	2,325,000
Total Stockholders' Equity	$9,825,000	$9,825,000	$9,825,000
Shares Outstanding	500,000	550,000	1,500,000
Book Value per Share *	$19.65	$17.86	$6.55

* See book value explanation under "Stockholders' Equity Section of Balance Sheet."

Stockholders' Equity Section of Balance Sheet

Preferred stock, common stock, additional paid-in-capital, retained earnings, and treasury stock are all reported on the balance sheet in the stockholders' equity section. Information regarding the par value, authorized shares, issued shares, and outstanding shares must be disclosed for each type of stock. If a company has preferred stock, it is listed first in the stockholders' equity section due to its preference in dividends and during liquidation.

Grandpa's Hook Rugs, Inc.
Partial Balance Sheet
As of December 31, 20X0

Preferred Stock, $100 par value, 10,000 shares authorized, issued and outstanding	$ 1,000,000
Common Stock, $1 par value, 2,000,000 shares authorized, 1,200,000 shares issued, and 1,180,000 shares outstanding	1,200,000
Additional Paid-in-Capital	16,800,000
Retained Earnings	3,670,000
Less: Treasury Stock, 20,000 shares	(240,000)
Total Stockholders' Equity	$22,430,000

Book value

Book value measures the value of one share of common stock based on amounts used in financial reporting. To calculate book value, divide total common stockholders' equity by the average number of common shares outstanding.

$$\text{Book Value} = \frac{\text{Total common stockholders' equity}}{\text{Average number of common shares outstanding}}$$

If preferred stock exists, the preferred stockholders' equity is deducted from total stockholders' equity to determine the total common stockholders' equity. The preferred stockholders' equity is the call price for the preferred stock plus any cumulative dividends in arrears. The par value is used if the preferred stock does not have a call price. Using Grandpa's Hook Rug, Inc. balance sheet information, the book value is:

$$\$18.16 = \frac{\$22,430,000 \ - 1,000,000 \ \text{perferred stockholders}' \ \text{equity}}{1,180,000 \ \text{shares outstanding}}$$

The $1,000,000 deducted from total stockholders' equity represents the par value of the preferred stock as the preferred stock is not callable. There was no common stock activity during the year. The book value of common stock is rarely identical to the market value. If the market value of asset is substantially different from their respective book values, then the book value per share measure loses most of its relevance.

Income Statement

The income statement of a corporation includes the same types of revenues and expenses as companies organized as sole proprietors and partnerships with one difference. A corporation is a legal entity and therefore, it must pay taxes. The expense for federal and state income taxes is shown on the income statement after other income/(expense), net (the nonoperating income and expenses) as follows:

Operating income	$92,500
Other income/(expense), net	
Interest revenue	5,000
Loss on sale of equipment	(2,400)
Interest expense	(8,000)
Income before taxes	87,100
Income tax expense	33,098
Net income	$54,002

Some companies report additional items after income tax expense on their income statements. These items represent special items outside of normal business operations. They are shown separately to ensure users can identify what income from continuing business results will be. If any special items are included on the income statement, the income tax expense or savings related to each item is net against the special item to report it after taxes. These additional special items may be one of three types: discontinued operations, extraordinary items, and changes in accounting principles.

Discontinued operations occur when a significant segment of a business has been identified for disposal. Once so identified, any gain or loss from operations of the segment while it is being disposed of and any gain or loss on the sale of the assets of the segment, are reported separately from the remaining, continuing operations.

Extraordinary items are events that occur infrequently and are unusual. They can include acts of God as long as they rarely occur in the area where the business operates. Events that would not be extraordinary as they occur regularly, although not yearly, are a severe freeze effecting crops in Florida or an earthquake in southern California.

A **change in accounting principle** occurs when a company changes from one acceptable principle to another. The new principle is used to calculate the current year's amounts in the financial statements. The effect of the change on any prior years' amounts is shown separately in the income statement, net of taxes. A partial income statement for a corporation with these items follows:

Income before taxes		$87,100
Income tax expense (38%)		<u>33,098</u>
Income from continuing operations		54,002
Discontinued operations		
Loss on operation of food divisions, net of $5,700 tax savings	(9,300)	
Gain on sale of food divisions, net of $9,500 income taxes	<u>15,500</u>	<u>6,200</u>
Income before extraordinary item and cumulative effect of accounting change		60,202
Extraordinary item		
Loss due to floods, net of $19,000 tax saving		(31,000)
Cumulative effect of change in accounting principle		
Effect on prior years of change in depreciation methods, net of $11,400 tax savings		<u>(18,600)</u>
Net income		<u>$10,602</u>

Earnings per share

Corporations are also required to report earnings per share on the income statement. **Earnings per share** represents the amount of earnings related to one share of common stock. There are two types of earnings per share, basic earnings per share and diluted earnings per share. If applicable, both types of earnings per share must be reported. In addition, if the corporation has any of the special items just described, earnings per share must be reported for income from continuing operations, each special item, and net income.

If no preferred stock is outstanding, basic earnings per share is calculated by dividing net income by weighted average number of common shares outstanding for the period.

$$\text{Basic Earnings Per Share} = \frac{\text{Net income}}{\text{Weighted average common shares outstanding}}$$

If preferred stock is outstanding, the current year's dividend declared on preferred stock is deducted from net income prior to dividing by weighted average number of common shares outstanding.

$$\begin{array}{c}\text{Basic Earnings Per Share} = \\ \text{if preferred stock}\end{array} \frac{\text{Net income} - \text{Preferred dividends}}{\begin{array}{c}\text{Weighted average number of common}\\\text{shares outstanding}\end{array}}$$

If the number of common shares outstanding changes during the period, the weighted average number of shares is used to calculate earnings per share. The weighting is based on how long shares are outstanding during the period. For example, if Tom & Margaret, Inc. began the year with 20,000 shares outstanding and issued an additional 5,400 shares on August 20, the weighted average shares would be calculated as:

$$20,000 \text{ shares } \times 12/12 = 20,000 \quad \text{outstanding entire year}$$

$$+ \quad 5,400 \text{ shares } \times \quad 5/12 = \underline{2,250} \quad \text{outstanding last 5 months}$$

$$\text{Weighted average shares} \quad \underline{22,250}$$

Alternatively, the weighted average shares may be calculated using the total common shares outstanding at a given time.

$20,000$ shares $\times$ $7/12$ $=$ $11,667$ outstanding entire year

$+ 25,400$ shares $\times$ $5/12$ $=$ $\underline{10,583}$ outstanding last 5 months

Weighted average shares $\underline{22,250}$

Diluted earnings per share
Diluted earnings per share uses the same formula. However, it requires that additional common shares, which could become outstanding as a result of the corporation's compensation plans or having issued convertible debt or convertible preferred stock, to also be included as outstanding common stock. As the formula includes additional shares outstanding, the diluted earnings per share is usually less than basic earnings per share.

Think of earnings per share as a continuum with basic earnings per share on one end and diluted earnings per share on the other. Further discussion of diluted earnings per share may be found in more advanced accounting books.

Companies may have cash balances that exceed their current operating needs. If the extra cash is not needed for a short period of time, the company may invest the excess cash to generate interest or dividend revenue. A company may also have a strategic purpose for accumulating cash, such as acquiring stock in another corporation. The investment of cash in each of these circumstances results in an investment being reported on the balance sheet. Investments are usually reported on a separate line from cash and may appear as short-term or long-term assets depending on the type of investment and management's plan for keeping the investment.

In choosing an investment, a company has many choices, including certificates of deposit, U.S. Treasury bills, bonds and notes, mutual funds, bonds of other companies, and stock of other companies. The types of accounting entries made are different for investments in bonds and stocks.

Accounting for Debt Securities

A **debt security** is an investment in bonds issued by the government or a corporation. At the time of purchasing a bond, the acquisition costs are recorded in an asset account, such as "Debt Investments." Acquisition costs include the market price paid for the bond and any investment fees or broker's commissions. For example, if Computers Galore purchases five of the 10%, ten-year $1,000 bonds issued by VEI on July 1 for $5,500 and pays broker's fees of $50, the entry to record the purchases would include both the purchase price and broker's fees in the cost of the investment.

General Journal

Date	Account Title and Description	Ref.	Debit	Credit
20X0				
July 1	Debt Investments		5,550	
	Cash			5,550
	Purchase of five VEI bonds			

The bonds pay interest every December 31 and June 30. When the semiannual interest is received on December 31, the entry to record it increases (debits) cash and increases (credits) interest revenue for $250 ($5,000 \times 10\% \times \frac{6}{12}$).

General Journal

Date	Account Title and Description	Ref.	Debit	Credit
20X0				
Dec. 31	Cash		250	
	Interest Revenue			250
	Interest on VEI bonds			

The bonds may be held to maturity or sold. If they are held to maturity, the bonds are classified as a long-term investment and the difference between the maturity value and the cost of the bonds is amortized to the income statement over the life of the bonds. If the bonds are held for sale (not held for maturity), their value changes as the market changes. (See "Balance Sheet Classification and Valuation" in this chapter.) At the time of the sale, a gain or loss is recorded for the difference between the book value and the proceeds received from the sale. For example, if one of the bonds was sold for $1,050 on June 1, the entry would include a loss of $60, the difference between the cost of $1,110 ($5,550 total acquisition cost divided by 5 bonds acquired) and the proceeds of $1,050.

General Journal

Date	Account Title and Description	Ref.	Debit	Credit
20X1				
June 1	Cash		1,050	
	Loss on Sale of Debt Investments		60	
	Debt Investments			1,110
	Sale of one VEI bond			

Accounting for Equity Securities

An **equity security** is an investment in stock issued by another company. The accounting for an investment in an equity security is determined by the amount of control of and influence over operating decisions the company purchasing the stock has over the company issuing the stock. If less than 20% of the stock is acquired and no significant influence or control exists, the investment is accounted for using the **cost method**. If 20–50% of the stock is owned, the investor is usually able to significantly influence the company it has invested in. Assuming the investor does not control the number of positions on the Board of Directors or hold key officer positions, this investment would be accounted for using the **equity method**. If the investor has 50% or more of a company's stock, significant influence and control are deemed to exist and the investor reports its results using **consolidated financial statements**. Although percent of voting stock owned serves as a guideline, the amount of influence and control is used to determine the accounting for equity securities.

Cost method

The cost method of accounting for stock investments records the acquisition costs in an asset account, "Equity Investments." As with debt investments, acquisition costs include commissions and fees paid to acquire the stock. If 72 shares of PWC Corporation are acquired when the market price is $28 and a $25 broker's fee is paid, the entry to record the purchase is:

General Journal

Date	Account Title and Description	Ref.	Debit	Credit
20X0				
Jan. 18	Equity Investments [(72 shares × $28) + $25]		2,041	
	Cash			2,041
	Acquire 1% of PWC Corporation stock			

As dividends are received, dividend income is recorded. If PWC Corporation pays a $1 per share cash dividend, the entry to record the receipt of the dividend increases (debits) cash and increases (credits) dividend revenue.

General Journal

Date	Account Title and Description	Ref.	Debit	Credit
20X0				
Mar. 12	Cash		72	
	Dividend Revenue			72
	Dividends received			

Equity investments accounted for by using the cost method are classified as either trading securities or available-for-sale securities, and the value of the investment is adjusted to market value. (See "Balance Sheet Classification and Valuation" in this chapter.) When an equity investment accounted for under the cost method is sold, a gain or loss is recognized for the difference between its acquisition cost and the proceeds received from the sale. Assume 36 of the PWC Corporation shares purchased were sold for $30 per share and a fee of $25 was paid. The entry to record the sale would increase (debit) cash for the proceeds received of $1,055 ($36 × $30 = $1,080 – $25 fee), decrease (credit) equity investments by $1,020.60 ($2,041 ÷ 72 = $28.35 × 36 shares) and record a gain on the sale for the $34.40 difference.

General Journal

Date	Account Title and Description	Ref.	Debit	Credit
20X0				
May 27	Cash		1,055	
	Equity Investments			1,020.60
	Gain on Sale of Equity Investments			34.40
	Sale of 36 share of PWC Corporation			

Equity method

The equity method of accounting for stock investments is used when the investor is able to significantly influence the operating and financial policies or decisions of the company it has invested in. Given this influence, the investor adjusts the value of its equity investment for dividends received from, and the earnings (or losses) of, the corporation whose stock has been purchased. The dividends received are accounted for as a reduction of the investment value because dividends are a partial return of the investor's investment. Assume The Sisters, Inc. acquired 30% of the stock of 2005 GROUP for $72,000 on Jan. 1. During the year, 2005 GROUP paid dividends totaling $30,000 and had net income of $150,000. Under the equity method, the $9,000 in dividends ($30,000 × 30%) received by The Sisters, Inc. would decrease the Investment in 2005 GROUP account rather than be reported as dividend revenue. The same account would increase $45,000 for The Sisters, Inc. 30% share of net income ($150,000 × 30%) as they treat their share of net income as revenue. At the end of the year, the balance in the Investment in 2005 GROUP account would be $108,000.

Investment in 2005 GROUP

Investment	72,000	9,000 Dividends Received
Share of net income	45,000	
	108,000	

The entries by The Sisters, Inc. to record the acquisition of 2005 GROUP stock, receipt of dividends, and share of net income are:

General Journal

Date	Account Title and Description	Ref.	Debit	Credit
20X0				
Jan. 1	Investment in 2005 GROUP		72,000	
	Cash			72,000
	Acquire 30% of 2005 GROUP stock			
Dec. 31	Cash		9,000	
	Investment in 2005 GROUP			9,000
	Dividends received– 2005 GROUP			
Dec. 31	Investment in 2005 GROUP		45,000	
	Revenue from Investment in 2005 GROUP			45,000
	Share of net income— 2005 GROUP			

Consolidated financial statements

A company that owns greater than 50% of another entity is called the **parent company**. The company whose stock is owned is called the **subsidiary company**. A parent company uses the equity method to account for its investment in its subsidiary. When financial statements are prepared, the assets and liabilities (balance sheet), revenues and expenses (income statement), and cash flows (cash flow statement) of both the parent company and subsidiary company are combined and shown in the same statements. These statements are called consolidated balance sheets, consolidated income statements, and consolidated cash flow statements—together they are called consolidated financial statements—and represent the financial position, results of operations, and cash flows of the parent company and any other companies it controls.

Balance Sheet Classification and Valuation

Debt investments and equity investments recorded using the cost method are classified as trading securities, available-for-sale securities, or, in the case of debt investments, held-to-maturity securities. The classification is based on the intent of the company as to the length of time it will hold each investment. A debt investment classified as **held-to-maturity** means the business has the intent and ability to hold the bond until it matures. The balance sheet classification of these investments as short-term (current) or long-term is based on their maturity dates.

Debt and equity investments classified as **trading securities** are those which were bought for the purpose of selling them within a short time of their purchase. These investments are considered short-term assets and are revalued at each balance sheet date to their current fair market value. Any gains or losses due to changes in fair market value during the period are reported as gains or losses on the income statement because, by definition, a trading security will be sold in the near future at its market value. In recording the gains and losses on trading securities, a valuation account is used to hold the adjustment for the gains and losses so when each investment is sold, the actual gain or loss can be determined. The valuation account is used to adjust the value in the trading securities account reported on the balance sheet. For example if the Brothers Quartet, Inc. has the following investments classified as trading securities, an adjustment for $9,000 is necessary to record the trading securities at their fair market value.

Valuation of Trading Securities

	Cost	Fair Market Value	Unrealized Gain (Loss)
XYZ Bonds	$25,000	$24,000	$(1,000)
ABC Stock	65,000	75,000	10,000
Total Trading Securities	$90,000	$99,000	$9,000

The entry to record the valuation adjustment is:

General Journal

Date	Account Title and Description	Ref.	Debit	Credit
20X0				
Dec. 31	Trading Securities Market Value Adjustment		9,000	
	Unrealized Gains and Losses Trading Securities			9,000
	Adjust trading securities to market value			

Debt and equity investments that are not classified as trading securities or held-to-maturity securities are called **available-for-sale securities**. Whereas trading securities are short-term, available-for-sale securities may be classified as either short-term or long-term assets based on management's intention of when to sell the securities. Available-for-sale securities are also valued at fair market value. Any resulting gain or loss is recorded to an unrealized gain and loss account that is reported as a separate line item in the stockholders' equity section of the balance sheet. The gains and losses for available-for-sale securities are not reported on the income statement until the securities are sold. Unlike trading securities that will be sold in the near future, there is a longer time before available-for-sale securities will be sold, and therefore, greater potential exists for changes in the fair market value. For example, assume the Brothers Quartet has available-for-sale securities, whose cost and fair market value are:

Valuation of Available-for-Sale Securities

	Cost	Fair Market Value	Unrealized Gain (Loss)
TLM Bonds	$ 40,000	$ 38,000	$(2,000)
EAK Stocks	50,000	70,000	20,000
MJM Stocks	25,000	22,000	(3,000)
Total Available-for-Sale Securities	$115,000	$130,000	$15,000

The entry to record the valuation adjustment is:

General Journal

Date	Account Title and Description	Ref.	Debit	Credit
20X0				
Dec. 31	Available-for-Sale Securities Market Value Adjustment		15,000	
	Unrealized Gains and Losses Available-for-Sale Securities			15,000
	Adjust available-for-sale securities to market value			

In the balance sheet the market value of short-term available-for-sale securities is classified as short-term investments, also known as marketable securities, and the unrealized gain (loss) account balance of $15,000 is considered a stockholders'equity account and is part of comprehensive income. When the balance is a net loss, it is subtracted from stockholders'equity.

A partial balance sheet for Brothers Quartet, showing the current assets and the stockholders' equity sections, follows:

Brother's Quartet
Partial Balance Sheet
As of December 31, 20X0

Assets	
Current assets	
Cash and cash equivalents	$ 30,000
Short-term investments	130,000
Accounts receivable, net of allowance	35,200
Merchandise inventory	29,600
Total Current Assets	$224,800
Stockholder's Equity	
Common Stock	$ 100,000
Additional Paid-in-Capital	400,000
Retained Earnings	563,000
Unrealized Gains on Investments	15,000
Total Stockholder's Equity	$1,078,000

Cash management is an important function for every business. Knowing what cash is expected to be received and what cash is required for payments is critical information in determining whether a company has excess cash for investment or will need additional cash to meet operating needs such as paying its employees or its suppliers.

The financial statement that reports activity in cash and cash equivalents for a period of time is called the **statement of cash flows**. **Cash equivalents** are highly liquid, short-term investments that usually mature within three months of their purchase. U.S. Treasury bills, money market funds, and commercial paper are usually classified as cash equivalents. In this discussion when cash is used, it refers to cash and cash equivalents.

Statement of Cash Flows Sections

The statement of cash flows has four main sections: Three are used to classify the types of cash inflows and outflows during the period and the fourth reconciles the total cash balance from the beginning to the end of the period. A skeleton outline of the statement of cash flows would look like this:

Name of Company
Statement of Cash Flows
For the Period Ended _____

Cash provided by (used by) operating activities
Cash provided by (used by) investing activities
Cash provided by (used by) financing activities   _____
Net increase (decrease) in cash and cash equivalents
Beginning cash and cash equivalents   _____

Ending cash and cash equivalents   =========

As with all statements, the statement of cash flows has a three-line heading stating the name of the company, the name of the statement, and the time period being reported on the statement (for example, month, quarter, year) with the period end date. The three sections of the statement are the operating, investing, and financing activities.

Operating activities

The first section is **operating activities**. This section tells the reader whether or not the company generated cash from its day-to-day operations. These activities include cash collections from customers, payments to employees and suppliers, tax payments, the receipt of interest and dividends and interest paid. There are two acceptable methods of reporting operating activities. Each method is discussed under the topic "Preparing the Statement of Cash Flows."

Investing activities

The second section is **investing activities**, which reflects how the company is using cash to grow/maintain its business. This section reports the activity in long-term asset accounts, such as land, buildings, equipment, intangible assets, and investments (excluding those classified as cash equivalents). If a company has collections from long-term notes receivable, they are reported as operating cash flows if the note receivable resulted from a sale to a customer, or investing cash flows if the note was taken for another purpose. Typical investing activities include the purchase and sale of equipment, purchase and sale of securities, and making and collecting loans.

Financing activities

In the third section, **financing activities**, the reader learns how the company chose to pay for its growth. Financing activities reports the activity in the long-term liability and stockholders' equity accounts. Typical financing activities are receipt and payment of loans, issuance of stock, payment of dividends, and repurchase of the company's stock.

In reporting the changes in cash in the investing and financing activities sections, each type of cash inflow or outflow is shown separately in the statement. For example, if the company sold equipment for $7,000 cash and purchased equipment for $50,000, the statement would report these two activities separately. Similarly, if the company borrows $1,000,000 and repays $150,000 during the period, these activities are reported separately. See Table 6-1 for major classifications of cash flow by category.

Cash reconciliation

The fourth section, the **cash reconciliation**, begins with the net change (increase or decrease) in cash that is the total of the operating, investing, and financing activities sections. The beginning of the period cash balance is added to the net change to obtain the ending cash balance. The ending cash balance is the same as cash on the balance sheet as of the end of the period.

Although the statement excludes non-cash transactions, significant non-cash transactions must be disclosed to the reader either below the statement or in the notes to the financial statements.

Table 6-1:
Summary of Typical Business Activities by
Statement of Cash Flow Section

	Cash Receipts	*Cash Payments*
Operating Activities	Collections from credit customers	Wages and salaries paid to employees
	Cash sales to customers	Payments to suppliers
	Interest from notes receivable, investments, or bank accounts	Payments for operating expenses, including donations
	Dividends received from investments in other companies	Payments for interest
	Tax refunds received	Payments for taxes
Investing Activities	Proceeds from sale of land, building, or equipment	Purchase of land, building, or equipment
	Proceeds from sale of debt or equity securities of another company	Purchase of debt or equity securities of another company
	Proceeds from sale of intangible assets	Purchase of intangible assets
	Principal repayments by employees and directors of loans made by company	Payments to loan money to non-customers

	Cash Receipts	Cash Payments
Financing Activities	Borrowed money	Repayments of loans and notes
	Proceeds from sale of company's own stock	Repurchase of company's stock
		Payment of dividends

Preparing the Statement of Cash Flows

There are two acceptable methods for reporting a statement of cash flows: the direct and the indirect methods. The difference between the two methods is seen in the operating section of the statement of cash flows. Although the total cash provided (used by) operating activities will be the same, the line items used to report the cash flows will be different.

Direct Method

Using the **direct method** requires cash related to day-to-day business operations to be identified by type of activity. For example, cash collected from customers, cash paid to employees, cash paid to suppliers (or paid for merchandise), cash paid for building operations, cash paid for interest, and cash paid for taxes. These types of labels make it easy for the reader to understand where cash came from and what it was spent on.

Indirect Method

Although the Financial Accounting Standards Board favors the direct method for preparing the statement of cash flows, most companies do not use the direct method, opting instead for the indirect method because it is easier to prepare and provides less detailed information to competitors. The **indirect method** begins with the assumption that net income equals cash and adjusts net income for significant non-cash income statement items such as depreciation, amortization, and gains and losses from sales, and for net changes in current asset, current liability, and income tax accounts. Table 6-2 shows the operating activities section prepared using each method.

Table 6-2:
Computation of Net Cash Flow Provided
by Operating Activities

Direct Method		Indirect Method	
Operating Activities		Operating Activities	
Collections from customers	$129,663	Net income	$ 6,300
Payments to suppliers	(71,976)	Adjustments to reconcile cash	
Payments for operating expenses	(29,317)	Depreciation expense	14,400
Payments for income taxes	(4,200)	Loss on sale of equipment	3,000
Payments for interest	(1,950)	Changes in Current Accounts	
		Decrease in accounts receivable	663
		Increase in inventory	(107)
		Increase in prepaid expenses	(142)
		Decrease in accounts payable	(919)

Direct Method		Indirect Method	
Operating Activities		Operating Activities	
		Increase in salaries payable	320
		Decrease in accrued expenses	(1,295)
Cash provided by operating activities	$22,220	Cash provided by operating activities	$22,220

The information in the 20X1 and 20X0 balance sheets and the 20X1 income statement for the Brothers' Quintet, Inc. will be used to illustrate the preparation of the statement of cash flows using the direct and indirect methods. Additional information regarding the Brothers' Quintet, Inc., include:

- All sales are made on credit. The company has no bad debts.

- Accounts payable represents amounts owed suppliers for merchandise. All purchases of merchandise are made on account.

- Equipment with a cost of $15,000 and accumulated depreciation of $5,000 was sold for $7,000.

- 1,000 additional shares of common stock were sold for $10 each.

- Dividends totaling $600 were declared and paid in the current year.

- No amounts are accrued for interest or income taxes.

Brothers' Quintet, Inc.
Balance Sheet As of December 31, 20X1 and 20X0

	20X1	20X0	Increase (Decrease)
ASSETS			
Current Assets			
Cash	$ 16,950	$ 6,330	$10,620
Accounts Receivable	18,567	19,230	(663)
Inventory	12,309	12,202	107
Prepaid Expenses	712	570	142
Total Assets	48,538	38,332	10,206
Property, Plant and Equipment			
Land	10,500	10,500	0
Building	50,000	50,000	0
Equipment	35,000	30,000	5,000
Less: Accumulated depreciation, building	(10,000)	(5,000)	(5,000)
Accumulated depreciation, equipment	(11,000)	(6,600)	(4,400)
Total property, plant and equipment	74,500	78,900	(4,400)
Other assets	1,500	1,500	0
Total Assets	$124,538	$118,732	$ 5,806

	20X1	20X0	Increase (Decrease)
LIABILITIES AND STOCKHOLDERS' EQUITY			
Current Liabilities			
Accounts payable	$ 15,730	$ 16,649	$ (919)
Wages payable	9,995	9,675	320
Accrued expenses	2,390	3,685	(1,295)
Total current liabilities	28,115	30,009	(1,894)
Long-term debt	15,000	23,000	(8,000)
Stockholders' Equity			
Common stock	30,000	20,000	10,000
Retained earnings	51,423	45,723	5,700
Total stockholders' equity	81,423	65,723	15,700
Total liabilities and stockholders' equity	$124,538	$118,732	$ 5,806

Brothers' Quintet, Inc.
Income Statement For the Year Ended December 31, 20X1

Sales, net	$129,000
Cost of goods sold	70,950
Gross profit	58,050
Operating expenses, includes depreciation expense of $14,400	42,600
Operating income	15,450
Interest expense	1,950
Loss on sale of equipment	3,000
Income before taxes	10,500
Income tax expense	4,200
Net income	$ 6,300

Direct Method of Preparing the Statement of Cash Flows

The discussion on the direct method of preparing the statement of
cash flows refers to the line items in the following statement and the
information previously given.

Brothers' Quintet, Inc.
Statement of Cash Flow
For the Year Ended December 31, 20X0

Operating Activities

Collections from customers	$129,663
Payments to suppliers	(71,976)
Payments for operating expenses	(29,317)
Payments for income taxes	(4,200)
Payments for interest	(1,950)
Cash provided by operating activities	22,220

Investing Activities

Purchase of equipment	$(20,000)
Proceeds from sale of equipment	7,000
Cash used by investing activities	(13,000)

Financing Activities

Proceeds from loan	4,000
Payments on loan	(12,000)
Proceeds from sale of stock	10,000

Operating Activities

Payment of dividends	(600)
Cash provided by financing activities	1,400
Net increase in cash	10,620
Beginning cash	6,330
Ending cash	$16,950

Preparing the statement of cash flows using the direct method would be a simple task if all companies maintained extremely detailed cash account records that could be easily summarized like this cash account:

Cash

Balance, beginning of year	6,330	71,976	Payments to suppliers
Collections from customers	129,663	30,517	Payments for operating expenses
Proceeds from equipment sale	7,000	3,000	Payments for income taxes
Proceeds from loan	4,000	1,950	Payments of interest
Proceeds from sale of stock	10,000	20,000	Purchase of equipment
		12,000	Payment on loan
		600	Payment of dividends
Balance, end of year	16,950		

Most companies record an extremely large number of transactions in their cash account and do not record enough detail for the information to be summarized. Therefore, the statement of cash flows is prepared by analyzing all accounts except the cash accounts. Remember that in accounting, all transactions affect at least two accounts. If cash increases or decreases, at least one other account also changes. If cash increases, that increase may also decrease another asset account, such as accounts receivable (payment from customer on account) or equipment (sale of equipment), or increase the sales account (cash sales). Similarly, if cash decreases, there may be an increase in another asset account, such as inventory (purchase of inventory) or equipment (purchase of equipment), a decrease in a liability account, such as accounts payable (payment to creditor) or notes payable (payment on loan), or an increase in an expense account (payment to vendor). Table 6-3 summarizes many cash activities and the related financial statement accounts used to analyze each listed activity.

Table 6-3:
Cash Activities and Corresponding
Financial Statement Accounts

Cash Flow Item	Balance Sheet Account(s)	Income Statement Account(s)
Cash collections from customers	Accounts receivable	Credit sales*
Cash sales to customers		Cash sales*
Proceeds from sale of equipment	Equipment Accumulated depreciation	Gain (loss) from sale of equipment
Proceeds from bank loan	Notes payable	
Proceeds from sale of stock	Common stock	
Payments to suppliers for merchandise	Inventory Accounts payable	Cost of goods sold
Payments for operating expenses**	Accrued expenses, including wages	Operating expenses
Payments for income taxes	Deferred income taxes	Income tax expense
Payments of interest	Interest payable	Interest expense
Purchase of equipment	Equipment	
Payment on loan	Notes payable	
Payment of dividends	Retained earnings	

* If separate cash sales and credit sales accounts are not maintained, there would be one line on the statement of cash flows labeled "cash from customers."

** Operating expenses excludes depreciation and amortization expense, non-cash items. The accounts related to depreciation and amortization are accumulated depreciation, accumulated amortization (or intangible asset) on the balance sheet, and depreciation or amortization expense on the income statement.

Operating activities

To prepare the operating activities section, certain accounts found in the current assets and current liabilities section of the balance sheet are used to help identify the cash flows received and incurred in generating net income.

Cash collections from customers. This consists of sales made for cash (cash sales) and cash collected from credit customers. The activity in the accounts receivable and sales accounts is used to determine the cash collections from customers. Accounts receivable decreased by $663 because the company received more cash from its customers than credit sales made by the company. The $663 decrease is added to sales per the income statement of $129,000 to determine the cash collections from customers reported in the cash flow statement of $129,663. If the accounts receivable balance had increased, the cash collected from customers would be determined by subtracting the increase in the accounts receivable balance from the sales balance because an increase in accounts receivable means your customers owe you the cash for their purchases (your sales).

Accounts Receivable			
Beginning balance	19,230		
Sales	129,000	129,663	Collections
Ending balance	18,567		

> Cash Received from Customers = Sales + Decrease in Accounts Receivable
> OR
> Sales – Increase in Accounts Receivable

Cash payments to suppliers. This represents the amount paid by the company for merchandise it plans to sell to its customers. It takes a two-step calculation to determine the cash payments to suppliers of $71,976. First, the $107 increase in the inventory account is added to the amount of cost of goods sold—found on the income statement—of $70,950 to get $71,057 as the cost of goods purchased.

An increase in inventory means a company purchased more than it sold. Because the amount paid for merchandise includes what was sold as well as what still remains on hand in inventory to be sold, the change in inventory effects the cash payments to suppliers. To determine the amount that has actually been paid for the merchandise purchased, a second step is needed. The decrease in accounts payable of $919 is then added to the amount of the purchases of $71,057 to calculate the cash paid to suppliers of $71,976. The decrease in accounts payable is added to the amount of the purchases because a decrease in the accounts payable balance means more cash was paid out than merchandise was purchased on credit.

If the inventory account balance had decreased, the decrease would be subtracted from the cost of goods sold to calculate the cost of goods purchased because the decrease indicates less merchandise was purchased than was sold during the period. If the accounts payable balance had increased, the amount of the increase would have been subtracted from the cost of goods purchased to determine cash payments to suppliers because the accounts payable increase means you have a loan from your suppliers and have not yet paid cash for your purchases.

Inventory

Beginning balance	12,202		
Purchases (1)	71,057	70,950	Cost of goods sold
Ending balance	12,309		

Accounts Payable

		16,649	Beginning balance
Payments	71,976	71,057	Purchases (1)
		15,730	Ending balance

Cash payments to suppliers =

(1) Cost of Purchases = Cost of Goods Sold + Increase in Inventory
OR
Cost of Goods Sold – Decrease in Inventory

And then

(2) Cash payments   Cost of Purchases + Decrease in Accounts Payable
     to suppliers =   OR
                   Cost of Purchases – Increase in Accounts Payable

Cash payments for operating expenses. This includes wages and other operating costs. To calculate the cash payments for operating expenses, two steps are required. First, the amount of total operating expenses in the income statement of $42,600 is reduced by $14,400 depreciation expense because depreciation is a non-cash expense. Second, the balance is adjusted for changes in the balances of related balance sheet accounts. For Brothers' Quintet, Inc., the related balance sheet accounts and the changes in these account balances are: increase of $142 in prepaid expenses; increase of $320 in wages payable; and $1,295 decrease in accrued expenses. The operating expenses before depreciation expense total $28,200. To this total the increase of $142 in prepaid expenses is added, the increase of $320 in wages payable is subtracted, and the decrease of $1,295 in accrued expenses is added to get cash payments to suppliers of $29,317. As with the prior calculations, the calculation changes with the direction of the change in the balances of the related balance sheet accounts. The operating expenses excluding depreciation expense would be decreased by a decrease in the prepaid expenses account's balance, increased by a decrease in the balance of the wages payable account, and decreased by an increase in the balance of the accrued expenses account.

Cash Paid for Operating Expenses =			
Operating Expenses (excluding depreciation expense)	+ Increase in Prepaid Expenses	– Increase in Wages Payable	+ Decrease in Accrued Expenses
	OR		
Operating Expenses (excluding depreciation expense)	– Decrease in Prepaid Expenses	+ Decrease in Wages Payable	– Increase in Accrued Expenses

Cash payments for income taxes. This represents amounts paid by the company for income taxes. The amount is calculated by taking income tax expense and increasing it by the amount of any decrease in the balance of the income taxes payable account or decreasing it by the amount of any increase in the balance of the income taxes payable account. In this case, there are no accrued taxes so the income tax expense is the same as cash paid for income taxes.

Cash Paid for Income Taxes =

Income Taxes Expense + Decrease in Income Taxes Payable
OR
Income Taxes Expense – Increase in Income Taxes Payable

Cash paid for interest. This represents amounts paid by the company for interest. The amount is calculated by taking interest expense and increasing it by the amount of any decrease in the balance of the interest payable account or decreasing it by the amount of an increase in the balance of the interest payable account. In this case, there is no balance in the accrued interest account at the end of the period so the cash paid for interest is the same as the interest expense.

Cash Paid for Interest =

Interest Expense + Decrease in Interest Payable
OR
Interest Expense − Increase in Interest Payable

Investing activities

To identify the investing activities, the long-term asset accounts must be analyzed.

Purchase of equipment. This includes the amount of cash paid for equipment. If a note had been taken in exchange for a portion of or all of the purchase price of the equipment, only the cash actually paid would be reported as a payment on the statement of cash flows. The portion of the purchase price represented by the note would be separately disclosed if it were a material amount.

Proceeds from sale of equipment (or any other long-term asset). The cash received from the sale is reported here. The proceeds are not adjusted for any gain or loss that may also have been recorded on the sale because only the proceeds represent cash, the gain or loss represents the difference between the book value of the assets and the value received. For the Brothers' Quintet, Inc., the book value is $10,000 ($15,000 cost − $5,000 accumulated depreciation). The loss is $3,000, calculated by subtracting the $10,000 book value from the proceeds of $7,000, and is reported in the income statement. The proceeds of $7,000 represent the actual cash received from the sale and is the amount reported in the statement of cash flows. The analysis of long-term asset accounts includes the following:

Building

Beg. Bal. 50,000	

Accumulated Depreciation – Building

	5,000 Beginning balance
	5,000 Depreciation expense
	10,000 Ending balance

Equipment

Beg. Bal. 30,000	
Purchase 20,000	15,000 Sale
End. Bal. 35,000	

Accumulated Depreciation – Equipment

	6,600 Beginning balance
Sale 5,000	9,400 Depreciation expense
	11,000 Ending balance

Loss on Sale of Equipment

3,000	

Financing activities

To identify the financing activities, the long-term liability accounts and the stockholders' equity accounts must be analyzed.

Proceeds for bank loan. Proceeds for bank loan of $4,000 represents additional borrowings during the year. Borrowings are not shown net of repayments. Each is treated as a separate activity to be reported on the statement of cash flows.

Payment on loan. Payment on loan of $12,000 equals the cash repayments made to the bank during the year.

Notes Payable	
	23,000 Beginning balance
Repayments 12,000	4,000 Additional loans
	15,000 Ending balance

Proceeds from sale of stock. This represents the cash received from the issuance of new shares to investors.

Common Stock	
	20,000 Beginning balance
	10,000 Issuance of stock
	30,000 Ending balance

Cash payments of dividends. This is the amount of dividends *paid* during the year. As the statement of cash flows includes only cash activity, the declaration of a dividend does not result in any reporting on the statement, it is only when the dividends are paid that they are included in the statement cash flows. In analyzing the retained earnings account, the other activity is the net income. The cash activities related to generating net income are included in the operating activities section of the statement of cash flows, and therefore, are not included in the financing activities section.

Retained Earnings

Dividends 600	45,723 Beginning balance
	6,300 Net income
	51,423 Ending balance

**Reconciliation of net income to cash provided
by (used by) operating activities**
If the direct method of preparing the statement of cash flows is used, the Financial Accounting Standards Board requires companies to disclose the reconciliation of net income to the net cash provided by (used by) operating activities that would have been reported if the indirect method had been used to prepare the statement.

Indirect Method of Preparing the Statement of Cash Flows

The discussion on the indirect method of preparing the statement of cash flows refers to the line items in the following statement and the information previously given about the Brothers' Quintet, Inc.

Brothers' Quintet, Inc.
Statement of Cash Flow
For the Year Ended December 31, 20X0

Operating Activities	
Net income	$ 6,300
Adjustments to reconcile to cash	
Depreciation expense	14,400
Loss on sale of equipment	3,000
Changes in current accounts	
Decrease in accounts receivable	663
Increase in inventory	(107)
Increase in prepaid expenses	(142)
Decrease in accounts payable	(919)
Increase in salaries payable	320
Decrease in accrued expenses	(1,295)
Cash provided by operating activities	22,220
Investing Activities	
Purchase of equipment	$(20,000)
Proceeds from sale of equipment	7,000
Cash used by investing activities	(13,000)
Financing Activities	
Proceeds from loan	4,000
Payments on loan	(12,000)

Proceeds from sale of stock	10,000
Payment of dividends	(600)
Cash provided by financing activities	1,400
Net increase in cash	10,620
Beginning cash	6,330
Ending cash	$16,950

Operating activities

Although the total cash provided by operating activities amount is the same whether the direct or indirect method of preparing the statement of cash flows is used, the information is provided in a different format.

The indirect method assumes everything recorded as a revenue was a cash receipt and everything recorded as an expense was a cash payment. Remember that under the accrual basis of accounting, revenues and expenses are recorded following the revenue recognition and matching principles which do not require cash receipts to record revenues or cash payments to record expenses. The operating activities section starts with net income per the income statement and adjusts it to remove the significant non-cash items.

Significant non-cash items on the income statement include depreciation and amortization expense and gains and losses from the sales of assets or retirement of debt. As depreciation expense and amortization expense are deducted in calculating net income (expenses are subtracted from revenues to determine net income), and depreciation and amortization expense do not result in cash payments by the company, depreciation expense and amortization expense are added back to net income.

Given the financial statements and information for the Brothers' Quintet, Inc., net income is $6,300. Net income first needs to be adjusted by significant non-cash items from the income statement: depreciation expense and the loss on the sale of the equipment.

Net income	$ 6,300
Adjustments to reconcile net income to cash	
Depreciation expense	14,400
Loss on sale of equipment	3,000

Next, net income is adjusted for the changes in most current asset, current liability, and income tax accounts on the balance sheet. The accounts receivable balance decreased $663 from $19,230 to $18,567. As cash is increased when cash is collected from customers, a decrease in the accounts receivable balance represents an increase in cash. Therefore, the $663 is added back to net income. If the accounts receivable balance increases, the amount of the increase is subtracted from net income, the opposite of what happens when the balance decreases. The inventory balance increased $107. As inventory is purchased, cash is assumed to be paid, so the $107 increase in the inventory balance is subtracted from net income (a decrease in the inventory balance would be added to net income). Similarly, the $142 increase in the prepaid expenses balance is also deducted from net income. The accounts payable balance decreased $919. When cash is paid to a supplier for purchases previously made on account, cash decreases. Thus, a decrease in the accounts payable balance represents a decrease in cash and the $919 decrease is subtracted from net income.

An increase in the accounts payable, or any current liability account balance is added to net income. The wages payable balance increased because a larger accrual was made to represent wages owed at the end of 20X1 than 20X0. Accrued wages are owed but not paid at the end of the month. An increase in a current liability account balance means cash has not been paid and therefore, the $320 increase in the wages payable balance is added to net income. The decrease in the accrued expenses balance of $1,295 is subtracted from net income. Once all of the changes in the current asset, current liability, and income tax accounts have been listed, the total cash provided by (used by) operating activities is determined by totaling all of the activity. Notice the amounts of any decreases are in parentheses.

Net income	$ 6,300
Adjustments to reconcile net income to cash	
Depreciation expense	14,400
Loss on sale of equipment	3,000
Changes in current accounts	
Decrease in accounts receivable	663
Increase in inventory	(107)
Increase in prepaid expenses	(142)
Decrease in accounts payable	(919)
Decrease in salaries payable	320
Decrease in accrued expenses	(1,295)
Cash provided by operating activities	$ 22,220

Investing activities and financing activities

The investing and financing sections of the statement of cash flows are prepared in the same way for the indirect method as previously discussed for the direct method.

Using the Statement of Cash Flow Information

The types of cash flows a company has, where cash comes from, and what it is used for provides insight into the financial stability of a company. The owners of three companies found the following information on their statement of cash flows:

	Mary Ellen	Louis	Lucille
Cash provided by (used by) operating activities	$10,000	$(50,000)	$60,000
Cash provided by (used by) investing activities			
Purchase of equipment		(100,000)	(28,000)
Proceeds from sale of equipment	30,000		
Cash provided by (used by) financing activities			
Proceeds from issuing debt		132,000	
Repayments of debt	(8,000)		
Proceeds from issuing stock		50,000	
Net increase in cash	$32,000	$ 32,000	$32,000

Although each company ended the year with a net increase in cash of $32,000, each company achieved that increase in a different way. If each of these businesses are in different industries or at different stages of their life cycle, the differences in the way the $32,000 was generated may not be a cause for concern. However, if each of these three companies are in the same industry and each has been in business for many years, it appears that the companies Mary Ellen and Lucille own may be in better financial condition than the one owned by Louis. Both Mary Ellen's and Lucille's companies had positive cash flow from operating activities. Louis' day-to-day operations resulted in a decrease of $50,000 in cash and because he purchased $100,000 of equipment, he had to finance these amounts by selling stock and borrowing from the bank.

Companies use their estimated cash flows to determine what to do with excess cash and whether or not they will need to borrow during a year. This enables the managers to plan for these needs before they have excess cash sitting in a bank account or have run out of cash and need to pay their employees. In addition to short-term cash needs, cash flow analysis is used for many business decisions, including for example, whether a company should invest in long-term assets, whether a part should be made or bought, and whether a new market should be opened. External users, such as suppliers, creditors, and potential investors, use the statement of cash flows when analyzing companies to decide whether to sell to, loan to, or invest in a company.

Need for Financial Statement Analysis

Financial statement analysis is used to identify the trends and relationships between financial statement items. Both internal management and external users (such as analysts, creditors, and investors) of the financial statements need to evaluate a company's profitability, liquidity, and solvency. The most common methods used for financial statement analysis are trend analysis, common-size statements, and ratio analysis. These methods include calculations and comparisons of the results to historical company data, competitors, or industry averages to determine the relative strength and performance of the company being analyzed.

The examples used in this discussion are based on The Home Project Company's financial statements found at the end of this chapter. *Note:* The amounts in the tables in each example are in thousands unless otherwise stated.

Trend Analysis

Trend analysis calculates the percentage change for one account over a period of time of two years or more.

Percentage change
To calculate the percentage change between two periods:

1. Calculate the amount of the increase/(decrease) for the period by subtracting the earlier year from the later year. If the difference is negative, the change is a decrease and if the difference is positive, it is an increase.

2. Divide the change by the earlier year's balance. The result is the percentage change.

Calculation of Percentage Change

	20X1	20X0	Increase/ (Decrease)	Percent Change
Cash	$ 6,950	$ 6,330	$ 620	9.8%
Accounts Receivable, net	18,567	19,330	(763)	(3.9%)
Sales	129,000	103,000	26,000	25.2%
Rent Expense	10,000	0	10,000	N/M
Net Income (Loss)	8,130	(1,400)	9,530	N/M

Calculation notes:

1. 20X0 is the earlier year so the amount in the 20X0 column is subtracted from the amount in the 20X1 column.

2. The percent change is the increase or decrease divided by the earlier amount (20X0 in this example) times 100. Written as a formula, the percent change is:

$$\% = \frac{20X1 \; amount - 20X0 \; amount}{20X0 \; amount} \times 100$$

3. If the earliest year is zero or negative, the percent calculated will not be meaningful. N/M is used in the above table for not meaningful.

4. Most percents are rounded to one decimal place unless more are meaningful.

5. A small absolute dollar item may have a large percentage change and be considered misleading.

Trend percentages
To calculate the change over a longer period of time—for example, to develop a sales trend—follow the steps below:

1. Select the base year.

2. For each line item, divide the amount in each nonbase year by the amount in the base year and multiply by 100.

3. In the following example, 20W7 is the base year, so its percentages (see bottom half of the table) are all 100.0. The percentages in the other years were calculated by dividing each amount in a particular year by the corresponding amount in the base year and multiply by 100.

Calculation of Trend Percentages

	20X1	20X0	20W9	20W8	20W7
Historical Data					
Inventory	$ 12,309	$12,202	$12,102	$11,973	$11,743
Property & equipment	74,422	78,938	64,203	65,239	68,450
Current liabilities	27,945	30,347	27,670	28,259	26,737
Sales	129,000	97,000	95,000	87,000	81,000
Cost of goods sold	70,950	59,740	48,100	47,200	45,500
Operating expenses	42,600	38,055	32,990	29,690	27,050
Net income (loss)	8,130	(1,400)	7,869	5,093	3,812
Trend Percentages					
Inventory	104.8	103.9	103.1	102.0	100.0
Property & equipment	108.7	115.3	93.8	95.3	100.0
Current liabilities	104.5	113.5	103.5	105.7	100.0
Sales	159.3	119.8	117.3	107.4	100.0
Cost of goods sold	155.9	131.3	105.7	103.7	100.0
Operating expenses	157.5	140.7	122.0	109.8	100.0
Net income (loss)	213.3	(36.7)	206.4	133.6	100.0

Calculation notes:

1. The base year trend percentage is always 100.0%. A trend percentage of less than 100.0% means the balance has decreased below the base year level in that particular year. A trend percentage greater than 100.0% means the balance in that year has increased over the base year. A negative trend percentage represents a negative number.

2. If the base year is zero or negative, the trend percentage calculated will not be meaningful.

In this example, the sales have increased 59.3% over the five-year period while the cost of goods sold has increased only 55.9% and the operating expenses have increased only 57.5%. The trends look different if evaluated after four years. At the end of 20X0, the sales had increased almost 20%, but the cost of goods sold had increased 31%, and the operating expenses had increased almost 41%. These 20X0 trend percentages reflect an unfavorable impact on net income because costs increased at a faster rate than sales. The trend percentages for net income appear to be higher because the base year amount is much smaller than the other balances.

Common-Size Analysis

Common-size analysis (also called **vertical analysis**) expresses each line item on a single year's financial statement as a percent of one line item, which is referred to as a base amount. The base amount for the balance sheet is usually total assets (which is the same number as total liabilities plus stockholders' equity), and for the income statement it is usually net sales or revenues. By comparing two or more years of common-size statements, changes in the mixture of assets, liabilities, and equity become evident. On the income statement, changes in the mix of revenues and in the spending for different types of expenses can be identified.

A common-size analysis for the latest two years of The Home Project Company is shown in the following example. To calculate the common-size for the 20X1 balance sheet, each amount was divided by $114,538, the "total asset" amount. For the 20X0 balance sheet, the common-size percentages were calculated by dividing by $118,732, "total assets." For the 20X1 income statement, each amount was divided by $129,000 the "sales, net" amount, and for the 20X0 income statement, each amount was divided by $97,000, the "sales, net" amount.

Calculation of Common-Size Analysis

	20X1		20X0	
	Amount	*Percent*	*Amount*	*Percent*
Balance Sheet				
Assets				
Current Assets				
Cash	$ 6,950	6.1	$ 6,330	5.3
Accounts receivable, net	18,567	16.2	19,230	16.2
Inventory	12,309	10.7	12,202	10.3
Prepaid expense	540	.5	532	.4
Total current assets	38,366	33.5	38,294	32.2
Property, plant & equipment, net	74,422	65.0	78,938	66.5
Other assets	1,750	1.5	1,500	1.3
Total assets	$114,538	100.0	$118,732	100.0

| | 20X1 | | 20X0 | |
	Amount	Percent	Amount	Percent
Liabilities and Stockholders' Equity				
Current Liabilities				
Accounts payable	$ 15,560	13.6	$ 16,987	14.3
Salaries payable	9,995	8.7	9,675	8.1
Accrued expenses	2,390	2.1	3,685	3.1
Total current liabilities	27,945	24.4	30,347	25.5
Long-term debt	15,000	13.1	23,000	19.4
Stockholders' equity	71,593	62.5	65,385	55.1
Total liabilities and stockholders' equity	$114,538	100.0	$118,732	100.0
Income Statement				
Sales, net	$129,000	100.0	$ 97,000	100.0
Cost of goods sold	70,950	55.0	59,740	61.6
Gross profit	58,050	45.0	37,260	38.4
Operating expenses	42,600	33.0	38,055	39.2
Operating income	15,450	12.0	(795)	(.8)
Interest expense	1,900	1.5	1,500	1.5
Income before income taxes	13,550	10.5	(2,295)	(2.3)
Income tax expense (benefit)	5,420	4.2	(895)	.9
Net income(loss)	$ 8,130	6.3	$ (1,400)	(1.4)

Ratio Analysis

Ratio analysis is used to evaluate relationships among financial statement items. The ratios are used to identify trends over time for one company or to compare two or more companies at one point in time. Financial statement ratio analysis focuses on three key aspects of a business: liquidity, profitability, and solvency.

Liquidity ratios

Liquidity ratios measure the ability of a company to repay its short-term debts and meet unexpected cash needs.

Current ratio. The **current ratio** is also called the working capital ratio, as working capital is the difference between current assets and current liabilities. This ratio measures the ability of a company to pay its current obligations using current assets. The current ratio is calculated by dividing current assets by current liabilities.

$$\text{Current Ratio} = \frac{\text{Current Assets}}{\text{Current Liabilities}}$$

	20X1	20X0
Current assets	$38,366	$38,294
Current liabilities	27,945	30,347
Current ratio	1.4 : 1	1.3 : 1

This ratio indicates the company has more current assets than current liabilities. Different industries have different levels of expected liquidity. Whether the ratio is considered adequate coverage depends on the type of business, the components of its current assets, and the ability of the company to generate cash from its receivables and by selling inventory.

Acid-test ratio. The **acid-test ratio** is also called the **quick ratio**. **Quick assets** are defined as cash, marketable (or short-term) securities, and accounts receivable and notes receivable, net of the allowances for doubtful accounts. These assets are considered to be very liquid (easy to obtain cash from the assets) and therefore, available for immediate use to pay obligations. The acid-test ratio is calculated by dividing quick assets by current liabilities.

$$\text{Acid-Test Ratio} = \frac{\text{Quick Assets}}{\text{Current Liabilities}}$$

	20X1	20X0
Cash	$ 6,950	$ 6,330
Accounts receivable, net	18,567	19,230
Quick Assets	$25,517	$25,560
Current Liabilities	$27,945	$30,347
Acid-test ratio	.9 : 1	.8 : 1

The traditional rule of thumb for this ratio has been 1:1. Anything below this level requires further analysis of receivables to understand how often the company turns them into cash. It may also indicate the company needs to establish a line of credit with a financial institution to ensure the company has access to cash when it needs to pay its obligations.

Receivables turnover. The **receivable turnover ratio** calculates the number of times in an operating cycle (normally one year) the company collects its receivable balance. It is calculated by dividing net credit sales by the average net receivables. Net credit sales is net sales less cash sales. If cash sales are unknown, use net sales. Average net receivables is usually the balance of net receivables at the beginning of the year plus the balance of net receivables at the end of the year divided by two. If the company is cyclical, an average calculated on a reasonable basis for the company's operations should be used such as monthly or quarterly.

$$\text{Receivables Turnover} = \frac{\text{Net Credit Sales}}{\text{Average Net Receivables}}$$

Calculation of Receivables Turnover

	20X1	20X0	20W9
Net credit sales	$129,000	$97,000	
Accounts receivable	18,567	19,230	$17,599
Average receivables	$(18,567+19,230)/2=$	$(19,230+17,599)/2=$	
	18,898.5	18,414.5	
Receivables turnover	$^{\$129,000}/_{\$18,898.5}=$	$^{\$97,000}/_{\$18,414.5}=$	
	6.8 times	5.3 times	

Average collection period. The **average collection period** (also known as **day's sales outstanding**) is a variation of receivables turnover. It calculates the number of days it will take to collect the average receivables balance. It is often used to evaluate the effectiveness of a company's credit and collection policies. A rule of thumb is the average collection period should not be significantly greater than a company's credit term period. The average collection period is calculated by dividing 365 by the receivables turnover ratio.

$$\text{Average Collection Period} = \frac{365 \text{ days}}{\text{Receivables Turnover}}$$

	20X1	20X0
Receivables Turnover	6.8 times	5.3 times
Average Collection Period	53.7 days	68.9 days

The decrease in the average collection period is favorable. If the credit period is 60 days, the 20X1 average is very good. However, if the credit period is 30 days, the company needs to review its collection efforts.

Inventory turnover. The **inventory turnover ratio** measures the number of times the company sells its inventory during the period. It is calculated by dividing the cost of goods sold by average inventory. Average inventory is calculated by adding beginning inventory and ending inventory and dividing by 2. If the company is cyclical, an average calculated on a reasonable basis for the company's operations should be used such as monthly or quarterly.

$$\text{Inventory Turnover Ratio} = \frac{\text{Cost of Goods Sold}}{\text{Average Inventory}}$$

Calculation of Inventory Turnover

	20X1	*20X0*	*20W9*
Cost of goods sold	$70,950	$59,740	
Inventory	12,309	12,202	$12,102
Average inventory	$(12,309+12,202)/2=$	$(12,202+12,102)/2=$	
	12,255.5	12,152	
Inventory turnover	$\$70,950/\$12,255.5 =$	$\$59,740/\$12,152=$	
	5.8 times	4.9 times	

Day's sales on hand. Day's sales on hand is a variation of the inventory turnover. It calculates the number of day's sales being carried in inventory. It is calculated by dividing 365 days by the inventory turnover ratio.

$$\text{Day's Sales on Hand} = \frac{365 \text{ days}}{\text{Inventory Turnover}}$$

	20X1	20X0
Inventory Turnover	5.8 times	4.9 times
Day's Sales on Hand	62.9 days	74.5 days

Profitability ratios

Profitability ratios measure a company's operating efficiency, including its ability to generate income and therefore, cash flow. Cash flow affects the company's ability to obtain debt and equity financing.

Profit margin. The **profit margin ratio**, also known as the operating performance ratio, measures the company's ability to turn its sales into net income. To evaluate the profit margin, it must be compared to competitors and industry statistics. It is calculated by dividing net income by net sales.

$$\text{Profit Margin} = \frac{\text{Net Income}}{\text{Net Sales}}$$

	20X1	20X0
Net income/(loss)	$ 8,130	$(1,400)
Net sales	129,000	97,000
Profit margin	6.3%	(1.4%)

Asset turnover. The **asset turnover ratio** measures how efficiently a company is using its assets. The turnover value varies by industry. It is calculated by dividing net sales by average total assets.

$$\text{Asset Turnover} = \frac{\text{Net Sales}}{\text{Average Total Assets}}$$

Calculation of Asset Turnover

	20X1	20X0	20W9
Net sales	$129,000	$ 97,000	
Total assets	114,538	118,732	$102,750
Average total assets	$(114,538+118,732)/_2=$	$(118,732+102,750)/_2=$	
	116,635	110,741	
Asset turnover	$^{\$129,000}/_{\$116,635}$ =	$^{\$97,000}/_{\$110,741}$ =	
	1.1 times	.9 times	

Return on assets. The **return on assets ratio (ROA)** is considered an overall measure of profitability. It measures how much net income was generated for each $1 of assets the company has. ROA is a combination of the profit margin ratio and the asset turnover ratio. It can be calculated separately by dividing net income by average total assets or by multiplying the profit margin ratio times the asset turnover ratio.

$$\text{Return on Assets} = \frac{\text{Net Income}}{\text{Average Total Assets}}$$

OR

$$\text{Return on Assets} = \text{Profit Margin} \times \text{Asset Turnover}$$

$$\frac{\text{Net income}}{\text{Average total assets}} = \frac{\text{Net Income}}{\text{Net Sales}} \times \frac{\text{Net Sales}}{\text{Average Total Assets}}$$

The information shown in equation format can also be shown as follows:

	20X1	20X0		20X1	20X0
Net income/ (loss)	$ 8,130	$(1,400)	Profit margin	6.3%	(1.4%)
Average total assets	116,635	110,741	Asset turnover	1.1 times	.9 times
Return on assets	6.97%	(1.3%)	Return on assets	6.93%*	(1.3%)

* Difference due to rounding.

Return on common stockholders' equity. The **return on common stockholders' equity** (ROE) measures how much net income was earned relative to each dollar of common stockholders' equity. It is calculated by dividing net income by average common stockholders' equity. In a simple capital structure (only common stock outstanding), average common stockholders' equity is the average of the beginning and ending stockholders' equity.

$$\text{Return on common stockholders' equity} = \frac{\text{Net Income}}{\text{Average Common Stockholders' Equity}}$$

Calculation of Return on Common Stockholders' Equity

	20X1	*20X0*	*20W9*
Net income/(loss)	$ 8,130	$ (1,400)	
Total stockholders' equity	71,593	65,385	$68,080
Average stockholders' equity	$(71,593+65,385)/2=$	$(65,385+68,080)/2=$	
	68,489	66,732.5	
Return on common stockholders' equity	$\$8,130/\$68,489=$	$\$(1,400)/\$66,732.5=$	
	11.9%	(2.1%)	

In a complex capital structure, net income is adjusted by subtracting the preferred dividend requirement, and common stockholders' equity is calculated by subtracting the par value (or call price, if applicable) of the preferred stock from total stockholders' equity.

$$\text{Return on Common Stockholders' Equity} = \frac{\text{Net Income} - \text{Preferred Dividends}}{\text{Average Common Stockholders' Equity}}$$

Earnings per share. Earnings per share (EPS) represents the net income earned for each share of outstanding common stock. In a simple capital structure, it is calculated by dividing net income by the number of weighted average common shares outstanding.

$$\text{Earnings Per Share} = \frac{\text{Net Income}}{\text{Weighted Average Common Shares Outstanding}}$$

Assuming The Home Project Company has 50,000,000 shares of common stock outstanding, EPS is calculated as follows:

	20X1	20X0	20W9
Net income/(loss)	$ 8,130	$ (1,400)	
Shares outstanding	50,000	50,000	50,000
Earnings/(loss) per share	$0.16	($0.03)	
Calculation notes:			

1. If the number of shares of common stock outstanding changes during the year, the weighted average stock outstanding must be calculated based on shares actually outstanding during the year. Assuming The Home Project Company had 40,000,000 shares outstanding at the end of 20X0 and issued an additional 10,000,000 shares on July 1, 20X1, the earnings per share using weighted average shares for 20X1 would be $0.18. The weighted average shares was calculated by 2 because the new shares were issued half way through the year.

$$\frac{\$8,130,000}{\left[\left(50,000,000 + 40,000,000\right)\right] \div 2} = \$0.18$$

2. If preferred stock is outstanding, preferred dividends declared should be subtracted from net income before calculating EPS.

Price-earnings ratio. The **price-earnings ratio (P/E)** is quoted in the financial press daily. It represents the investors' expectations for the stock. A P/E ratio greater than 15 has historically been considered high.

$$\text{Price-Earnings ratio} = \frac{\text{Market price per common share}}{\text{Earnings per share}}$$

If the market price for The Home Project Company was $6.25 at the end of 20X1 and $5.75 at the end of 20X0, the P/E ratio for 20X1 is 39.1.

	20X1	20X0
Market price per common share	$6.25	$5.75
Earnings per share	$0.16	(0.03)
P/E ratio	39.1	N/M

Payout ratio. The **payout ratio** identifies the percent of net income paid to common stockholders in the form of cash dividends. It is calculated by dividing cash dividends by net income.

$$\text{Payout Ratio} = \frac{\text{Cash Dividends}}{\text{Net Income}}$$

Cash dividends for The Home Project Company for 20X1 and 20X0 were $1,922,000 and $1,295,000, respectively, resulting in a payout ratio for 20X1 of 23.6%.

	20X1	20X0
Cash dividends	$1,922	$1,295
Net income/(loss)	8,130	(1,400)
Payout ratio	23.6%	N/M

A more stable and mature company is likely to pay out a higher portion of its earnings as dividends. Many startup companies and companies in some industries do not pay out dividends. It is important to understand the company and its strategy when analyzing the payout ratio.

Dividend yield. Another indicator of how a corporation performed is the **dividend yield**. It measures the return in cash dividends earned by an investor on one share of the company's stock. It is calculated by dividing dividends paid per share by the market price of one common share at the end of the period.

$$\text{Dividend Yield} = \frac{\text{Dividends Paid Per Share}}{\text{Market Price of One Share Common Stock at End of Period}}$$

	20X1	20X0
Cash dividends per share	$ .038	$ .026
Market price per common share	$6.25	$5.75
Dividend yield	0.6%	0.5%

A low dividend yield could be a sign of a high growth company that pays little or no dividends and reinvests earnings in the business or it could be the sign of a downturn in the business. It should be investigated so the investor knows the reason it is low.

Solvency ratios
Solvency ratios are used to measure long-term risk and are of interest to long-term creditors and stockholders.

Debt to total assets ratio. The **debt to total assets ratio** calculates the percent of assets provided by creditors. It is calculated by dividing total debt by total assets. Total debt is the same as total liabilities.

$$\text{Debt to total assets ratio} = \frac{\text{Total debt}}{\text{Total assets}}$$

	20X1	20X0
Current liabilities	$ 27,945	$ 30,347
Long-term debt	15,000	23,000
Total debt	$ 42,945	$ 53,347
Total assets	$114,538	$118,732
Debt to total assets	37.5%	44.9%

The 20X1 ratio of 37.5% means that creditors have provided 37.5% of the company's financing for its assets and the stockholders have provided 62.5%.

Times interest earned ratio. The **times interest earned ratio** is an indicator of the company's ability to pay interest as it comes due. It is calculated by dividing earnings before interest and taxes (EBIT) by interest expense.

$$\text{Times interest earned} = \frac{\text{Income* Before Interest Expense and Income Tax Expense (EBIT)}}{\text{Interest Expense}}$$

* also called earnings

	20X1	20X0
Income before interest expense and income taxes		
Income (loss) before taxes	$13,550	$(2,295)
Interest expense	1,900	1,500
EBIT	$15,450	$ (795)
Interest Expense	$ 1,900	$ 1,500
Times interest earned	8.1 times	N/M

A times interest earned ratio of 2–3 or more indicates that interest expense should reasonably be covered. If the times interest earned ratio is less than two it will be difficult to find a bank to loan money to the business.

Limitations on Financial Statement Analysis

Many things can impact the calculation of ratios and make comparisons difficult. The limitations include:

- The use of estimates in allocating costs to each period. The ratios will be as accurate as the estimates.

- The cost principle is used to prepare financial statements. Financial data is not adjusted for price changes or inflation/deflation.

- Companies have a choice of accounting methods (for example, inventory LIFO vs FIFO and depreciation methods). These differences impact ratios and make it difficult to compare companies using different methods.

- Companies may have different fiscal year ends making comparison difficult if the industry is cyclical.

- Diversified companies are difficult to classify for comparison purposes.

- Financial statement analysis does not provide answers to all the users' questions. In fact, it usually generates more questions!

The Home Project Company
Five-Year Financial Statements
(In thousands)

	20X1	20X0	20W9	20W8	20W7
Balance Sheet					
Assets					
Current Assets					
Cash	$ 6,950	$ 6,330	$ 6,835	$ 6,145	$ 5,987
Accounts receivable, net	18,567	19,230	17,599	17,230	17,114
Inventory	12,309	12,202	12,102	11,973	11,743
Prepaid expense	540	532	511	501	488
Total current assets	38,366	38,294	37,047	35,849	35,332
Property, plant & equipment, net	74,422	78,938	64,203	65,239	68,450
Other assets	1,750	1,500	1,500	1,500	1,500
Total assets	$114,538	$118,732	$102,750	$102,588	$105,282

	20X1	20X0	20W9	20W8	20W7
Liabilities and Stockholders' Equity					
Current Liabilities					
Accounts payable	$ 15,560	$ 16,987	$ 16,010	$ 16,919	$ 16,062
Salaries payable	9,995	9,675	9,175	8,750	8,450
Accrued expenses	2,390	3,685	2,485	2,590	2,225
Total current liabilities	27,945	30,347	27,670	28,259	26,737
Long-term debt	15,000	23,000	7,000	13,200	22,000
Stockholders' equity	71,593	65,385	68,080	61,129	56,545
Total liabilities and stockholders' equity	$114,538	$118,732	$102,750	$102,588	$105,282

The Home Project Company
Five-Year Income Statements
(in thousands)

	20X1	20X0	20W9	20W8	20W7
Sales, net	$129,000	$ 97,000	$ 95,000	$ 87,000	$ 81,000
Cost of goods sold	70,950	59,740	48,100	47,200	45,500
Gross profit	58,050	37,260	46,900	39,800	35,500
Operating expenses	42,600	38,055	32,990	29,690	27,050
Operating income	15,450	(795)	13,910	10,110	8,450
Interest expense	1,900	1,500	1,010	1,760	2,200
Income before income taxes	13,550	(2,295)	12,900	8,350	6,250
Income tax expense (benefit)	5,420	(895)	5,031	3,257	2,438
Net income(loss)	$ 8,130	$ (1,400)	$ 7,869	$ 5,093	$ 3,812

Financial statements are used by both external users and internal management and provide general information about the entire company. For example, the balance sheet reports total inventories and the income statement reports cost of goods sold, but the costs of individual products are not disclosed to the public. Internal management needs detailed information to make decisions about its business. A comparison of managerial and financial accounting shows the differences between the two sets of information.

Managerial and Financial Accounting Comparison

	Managerial Accounting	*Financial Accounting*
Users	Internal managers	Creditors, investors, analysts, and other external users
Guidelines for preparation	Flexible	GAAP—rigid
Purpose	Decision making and control information	General information for credit and investment decisions
Frequency of preparation	As needed	Annually and quarterly
Independent opinion	None required	Auditor's opinion
Type of information	Specific to project or management action—may be detailed and include estimates	General purpose—very few estimates

Manufacturing Financial Statements

Manufacturing companies have several different accounts compared to service and merchandising companies. These include three types of inventory accounts—raw materials, work-in-process, and finished goods—and several long-term fixed asset accounts. A manufacturing company uses purchased raw materials and/or parts to produce a product for sale. At a point in time, the company's inventories consist of **raw materials**, those materials and parts waiting to be used in production; **work-in-process**, all material, labor, and other manufacturing costs accumulated to date for products not yet completed; and **finished goods**, the cost of completed products that are ready to be sold. The value of each type of inventory is disclosed in a company's financial statements. The amounts may be shown individually on the face of the balance sheet or disclosed in footnotes.

In the long-term asset section of a manufacturing company's balance sheet, one would expect to find factory buildings and equipment and possibly a small tools account. A manufacturer often has patents for its products or processes. The capitalized costs associated with a patent would be included in the intangible asset section of the balance sheet. The income statement for a manufacturing company is similar to that prepared for a merchandising company. In calculating cost of goods sold, only the finished goods inventory account is used, as shown.

Manufacturer		Merchandiser	
Cost of goods sold		Cost of goods sold	
Beginning finished goods inventory	$ 14,500	Beginning merchandise inventory	$10,300
Cost of goods manufactured	255,000	Cost of goods purchased	129,200
Goods available for sale	269,500	Goods available for sale	139,500
Ending finished goods inventory	(12,600)	Ending inventory merchandise	(10,600)
Cost of goods sold	$256,900	Cost of goods sold	$128,900

Costing Terminology

Expenses on an income statement are considered product or period costs. **Product costs** are those costs assigned to an inventory account that eventually become part of cost of goods sold. Examples of manufacturing product costs are raw materials used, direct labor, factory supervisor's salary, and factory utilities. In a manufacturing company, product costs are also called **manufacturing costs**. In a service company, product costs are also accumulated as inventory (such as the cost of an audit or of a will). **Period costs** are those costs recorded as an expense in the period they are incurred. Selling expenses such as sales salaries, sales commissions, and delivery expense, and general and administrative expenses such as office salaries, and depreciation on office equipment, are all considered period costs. In a manufacturing company, these costs are often referred to as **non-manufacturing costs**. There are three categories of manufacturing costs: direct materials, direct labor, and overhead.

Direct materials are those materials (including purchased parts) that are used to make a product and can be directly associated with the product. Some materials used in making a product have a minimal cost, such as screws, nails, and glue, or do not become part of the final product, such as lubricants for machines and tape used when painting. Such materials are called **indirect materials** and are accounted for as manufacturing overhead. **Direct labor** is the cost of the workers who make the product. The cost of supervisory personnel, management, and factory maintenance workers, although they are needed to operate the factory, are classified as **indirect labor** because these workers do not use the direct materials to build the product. **Manufacturing overhead** costs include indirect materials, indirect labor, and all other manufacturing costs. Depreciation on factory equipment, factory rent, factory insurance, factory property taxes, and factory utilities are all examples of manufacturing overhead costs. Together, the direct materials, direct labor, and manufacturing overhead are referred to as **manufacturing costs**. The costs of selling the product are operating expenses (period cost) and not part of manufacturing overhead costs because they are not incurred to make a product.

The Cost of Goods Manufactured Schedule

The **cost of goods manufactured schedule** is used to calculate the cost of producing products for a period of time. The cost of goods manufactured amount is transferred to the finished goods inventory account during the period and is used in calculating cost of goods sold on the income statement. The cost of goods manufactured schedule reports the total manufacturing costs for the period that were added to work-in-process, and adjusts these costs for the change in the work-in-process inventory account to calculate the cost of goods manufactured.

Red Car, Inc.
Cost of Goods Manufactured Schedule
For the Year Ended December 31, 20X0

Direct materials used

Beginning raw materials inventory	$ 6,200	
Add: Cost of raw materials purchased	49,400	
Total raw materials available	55,600	
Less: Ending raw materials inventory	(5,800)	
Total raw materials used		$ 49,800
Direct labor		125,600
Manufacturing overhead		
Indirect materials	4,100	
Indirect labor	43,700	
Depreciation—factory building	9,500	
Depreciation—factory equipment	5,400	
Insurance—factory	12,000	
Property taxes—factory	4,500	
Total manufacturing overhead		79,200
Total manufacturing costs		254,600
Add: Beginning work-in-process inventory		10,200
		264,800
Less: Ending work-in-process inventory		(9,800)
Cost of goods manufactured		$255,000

The cost of goods manufactured for the period is added to the finished goods inventory. To calculate the cost of goods sold, the change in finished goods inventory is added to/subtracted from the cost of goods manufactured.

Red Car, Inc.
Income Statement
For the Year Ended December 31, 20X0

Sales				$427,000
Cost of goods sold				
Beginning finished goods inventory		$ 14,500		
Cost of goods manufactured		255,000		
Total goods available for sale		269,500		
Ending finished goods inventory		(12,600)		
Cost of goods sold			256,900	
Gross profit			170,100	
Operating expenses				
Selling expenses				
Sales salaries	$65,300			
Depreciation—sales equipment	21,000			
Total selling expenses		86,300		

Administrative expenses			
Office salaries	35,000		
Depreciation—office equipment	12,000		
Insurance expense	9,000		
Office supplies expense	2,400		
Total administrative expenses		58,400	
Total operating expenses			144,700
Income from operations			25,400
Interest revenue			5,100
Income before taxes			30,500
Income taxes			10,675
Net income			$ 19,825

Accounting by Manufacturing Companies

The accounting cycle is the same in a manufacturing company, merchandising company, and a service company. Journal entries are used to record transactions, adjusting journal entries are used to recognize costs and revenues in the appropriate period, financial statements are prepared, and closing entries are recorded. Raw material purchases are recorded in the raw material inventory account if the perpetual inventory method is used, or the raw materials purchases account if the periodic inventory method is used. For example, using the periodic inventory method, the purchase of $750 of raw materials on account is recorded as an increase (debit) to raw materials purchases and an increase (credit) to accounts payable.

General Journal

Date	Account Title and Description	Ref.	Debit	Credit
20X0				
May 27	Raw Materials Purchases		750	
	Accounts Payable—TLM Co.			750
	Purchase materials from TLM			

The entry to record payroll would include an increase (debit) to direct labor instead of wages expense and an increase (credit) to the withholding liability account and wages payable. To record $1,000 wages for T. Kaschalk, the entry would be:

General Journal

Date	Account Title and Description	Ref.	Debit	Credit
20X0				
May 31	Direct Labor		1,000	
	Federal Income Taxes Payable			150.00
	FICA Taxes Payable			76.50

Date	Account Title and Description	Ref.	Debit	Credit
	Credit Union Payable			50.00
	Wages Payable			723.50
	Record TK wages			

The factory building depreciation of $9,500 is classified as a manufacturing cost. It is recorded with an increase (debit) to factory depreciation and an increase (credit) to accumulated depreciation—building.

General Journal

Date	Account Title and Description	Ref.	Debit	Credit
20X0				
May 31	Factory Depreciation Expense		9,500	
	Accumulated Depreciation— Building			9,500
	Record factory building depreciation			

Some companies use one account, factory overhead, to record all costs classified as factory overhead. If one overhead account is used, factory overhead would be debited in the previous entry instead of factory depreciation.

At the end of the cycle, the closing entries are prepared. For a manufacturing company that uses the periodic inventory method, closing entries update retained earnings for net income or loss and adjust each inventory account to its period end balance. A special account called manufacturing summary is used to close all the accounts whose amounts are used to calculate cost of goods manufactured. The manufacturing summary account is closed to income summary. Income summary is eventually closed to retained earnings. The manufacturing accounts are closed first. The closing entries that follow are based on the accounts included in the cost of goods manufactured schedule and income statement for Red Car, Inc.

General Journal

Date	Account Title and Description	Ref.	Debit	Credit
C1	Raw Materials Inventory (Ending)		5,800	
	Work-in-Process Inventory (Ending)		9,800	
	Manufacturing Summary			15,600
	Adjust inventory balances			
C2	Manufacturing Summary		270,600	
	Raw Materials Inventory (Beginning)			6,200
	Work-in-Process Inventory (Beginning)			10,200
	Raw Materials Purchases			49,400
	Direct Labor			125,600
	Indirect Materials			4,100
	Indirect Labor			43,700
	Depreciation— Factory Building			9,500
	Depreciation— Factory Equipment			5,400
	Insurance—Factory			12,000
	Property Taxes—Factory			4,500
	Close manufacturing accounts and adjust inventory balances			

Date	Account Title and Description	Ref.	Debit	Credit
C3	Income Summary		255,000	
	Manufacturing Summary			255,000
	Close manufacturing summary			
C4	Finished Goods Inventory (Ending)		12,600	
	Sales		427,000	
	Interest Revenue		5,100	
	Income Summary			444,700
	Close revenue accounts and adjust inventory			
C5	Income Summary		169,875	
	Finished Goods Inventory (Beginning)			14,500
	Sales Salaries Expense			65,300
	Depreciation— Sales Equipment			21,000
	Office Salaries Expense			35,000
	Depreciation– Office Equipment			12,000

Date	Account Title and Description	Ref.	Debit	Credit
	Insurance Expense			9,000
	Office Supplies Expense			2,400
	Income Tax Expense			10,675
	Close operating expense accounts and adjust inventory			
C6	Income Summary		19,825	
	Retained Earnings			19,825
	Close income summary			

The following T-accounts illustrate the impact of the closing entries on the special closing accounts and retained earnings.

Manufacturing Summary

C2	270,600	15,600	C1
	255,000		
		255,000	C3
	0		

Income Summary

C3	255,000	444,700	C4
C5	169,875		
	424,875	444,700	
		19,825	
C6	19,825		
	0		

Retained Earnings

	19,825	C6

The two basic types of manufacturing processes are the job order approach, where each order is customized, and mass production, where the product is always the same. To accompany these procedures are the two traditional types of cost accounting systems: job order cost system and process cost system. The information captured by these cost accounting systems aids managers in determining total production costs.

Job Order Cost System

The **job order cost system** is used when products are made based on specific customer orders. Each product produced is considered a job. Costs are tracked by job. Services rendered can also be considered a job. For example, service companies consider the creation of a financial plan by a certified financial planner, or of an estate plan by an attorney, unique jobs. The job order cost system must capture and track by job the costs of producing each job, which includes materials, labor, and overhead in a manufacturing environment. To track data, the following documents are used:

- **Job cost sheet.** This is used to track the job number; customer information; job information (date started, completed, and shipped); individual cost information for materials used, labor, and overhead; and a total job cost summary. See Figure 9-1.

- **Materials requisition form.** To assure that materials costs are properly allocated to jobs in process, a materials requisition form (see Figure 9-2) is usually completed as materials are taken from the raw materials inventory and added to work-in-process.

- **Time ticket.** Labor costs are allocated to work-in-process inventory based on the completion of time tickets (see Figure 9-3) identifying what job a worker spent time on.

Predetermined overhead rate

Factory overhead costs are allocated to jobs in process using a predetermined overhead rate. The **predetermined overhead rate** is determined by estimating (during the budget process) total factory overhead costs and dividing these total costs by direct labor hours or direct labor dollars. For example, assume a company using direct labor dollars for the allocation of overhead estimated its total overhead costs to be $300,000 and total direct labor dollars to be $250,000. The company's predetermined overhead rate for allocating overhead to jobs in process is 120% of direct labor dollars, and is calculated as follows:

$$\text{Predetermined Overhead Rate} = \frac{\text{Total factory overhead costs}}{\text{Total direct labor costs}}$$

$$\text{Predetermined Overhead Rate} = \frac{\$300,000}{\$250,000} = 1.2 \; or \; 120\%$$

If direct labor costs are $20,000 for the month, overhead of $24,000 ($20,000 × 120%) would be allocated to work-in-process inventory. Factory overhead would be allocated to individual jobs based on the portion of the $20,000 direct labor cost that is assigned to each job. If job number 45 had $9,000 in direct labor cost for the month, factory overhead of $10,800 ($9,000 × 120%) would also be allocated to the job.

Once a job is completed, the total costs assigned to the job are transferred from work-in-process inventory to finished goods inventory. Once the job is sold and delivered, the job costs are transferred from finished goods inventory to cost of goods sold. Figure 9-4 summarizes the flow of costs in a job order cost system and Figure 9-5 summarizes the journal entries required given the flow of costs in Figure 9-4. The ending balances in the three inventory accounts would be reported as inventories on the balance sheet and cost of goods sold would be reported on the income statement.

The factory overhead account (see Figure 9-5) has a balance which indicates the amount of overhead applied to work-in-process inventory is different from the actual overhead incurred. When there is a debit balance in the factory overhead account, it is called under-applied overhead meaning not enough overhead was allocated to jobs. If the balance in the factory overhead account was a credit, the overhead would be over-applied, meaning too much overhead was allocated to jobs. Factory overhead must be zero at the end of the year. Most companies transfer the balance in factory overhead to cost of goods sold. An alternative method, although more complex, is to allocate the under- or over-applied balance among the work-in-process inventory, finished goods inventory, and cost of goods sold accounts. The $2,600 account balance in factory overhead in Figure 9-5 is relatively small. To zero out the account balance and transfer it to cost of goods sold, the entry would be:

General Journal

Date	Account Title and Description	Ref.	Debit	Credit
20X0				
Dec. 31	Cost of Goods Sold		2,600	
	Factory Overhead			2,600
	Transfer under-applied overhead			

SAMPLE JOB COST SHEET

Twin Publishers   Job 4401

Company: Vector Publishing Co.

Address: 1234 Main Street
                    East Detroit, MI 48021

Job requirements: 2,000 copies workbooks by 8/1

Date promised: 7/25   Date started: 6/15   Date finished: 7/13

Cost summary

Materials	$11,000
Labor	7,600
Overhead	11,400
Total	$30,000

Direct materials			Direct labor			Manufacturing Overhead		
Date	Requisition #	Cost	Date	Time Ticket	Cost	Date	Rate	Cost
6/15	R-1396	11,000	6/22	L-1034	1,000	7/13	150% of	11,400
			6/22	L-1035	1,000		direct labor	
			6/29	L-2955	1,000		cost	
			6/29	L-2956	1,000			
			7/6	L-3179	1,000			
			7/6	L-3180	1,000			
			7/13	L-2193	1,000			
			7/13	L-2194	600			
Total		11,000	Total		7,600	Total		11,400

Figure 9-1

SAMPLE MATERIALS REQUISITION

Twin Publishers Materials Requisition				R-1396
Date: 6/15		Job No. 4401		
Quantity	Item #	Item Description	Cost per unit	Total cost
220,000 sheets	15	white paper	.05	11,000
Requested by: LJM			Received by:	KLJM
	Salesman			Printing Department
			Costed by:	EAM
				Accounting Department

Figure 9-2

SAMPLE TIME TICKET

Twin Publishers Time Ticket

Employee: GMC Nic   Employee #: 2863

Job Worked On: 4401   Pay Date: 7/13

Date	Start	Stop	Total Hours	Hourly Rate	Total Cost
7/10	0800	1200	4	25	100
7/10	1300	1700	4	25	100
7/11	0800	1200	4	25	100
7/11	1300	1700	4	25	100
7/12	0800	1200	4	25	100
7/12	1300	1700	4	25	100
	Total				600

Approved by: MJM   Costed by: MJM
              Supervisor   Accounting Department

Figure 9-3

JOB ORDER COST SYSTEM COST FLOWS

Raw Materials Inventory			
purchase	A	B	direct material requisition
		D	indirect material requisition

Wages Payable			
paid wages	J	C	direct labor
		E	indirect labor

Factory Overhead			
indirect material	D	G	applied to jobs
indirect labor	E		
other	F		

Factory Overhead Subsidiary Ledger

Indirect Materials	Indirect Labor
D	E

Factory Utilities	Factory Rent
F	F

Work-in-Progress Inventory	
B	H
C	
G	

Work-in-Process Inventory Subsidiary Ledger

Job 100		Job 101		Job 102	
B	H	B	H	B	
C		C		C	
G		G		G	

Finished Goods Inventory	
H	I

Finished Goods Inventory Subsidiary Ledger

Job 99		Job 100		Job 101
B	I	H	I	H

Cost of Goods Sold	
I	

Cost of Goods Inventory Subsidiary Ledger

Job 99	
I	

Figure 9-4

Key:

A *Purchased raw materials*

B *Direct material requisition to be used on jobs*

C *Direct labor payroll based on time ticket*

D *Indirect materials used*

E *Indirect labor payroll*

F *Other overhead costs incurred*

G *Overhead applied to jobs (direct labor dollars ¥ 80% pre-determined overhead rate)*

H *Transfer completed jobs to finished goods inventory*

I *Transferred sold jobs to cost of goods sold*

J *Paid wages*

JOB ORDER COST SYSTEM COST FLOWS

Raw Materials Inventory			
beginning bal. 50,000	16,500	(B)	
(A)	15,000	5,700	(D)
ending bal.	42,800		

Wages Payable			
(J)	31,000	21,000	(C)
		10,000	(E)
		0	

Factory Overhead			
(D)	5,700	16,800	(G)
(E)	10,000		
(F)	3,700		
ending bal.	2,600		

Factory Overhead Subsidiary Ledger

Indirect Materials	Indirect Labor
(D) 5,700	(E) 10,000

Factory Utilities	Factory Rent
(F) 1,200	(F) 2,500

Work-in-Progress Inventory			
beginning bal. 6,200	45,200	(H)	
(B)	16,500		
(C)	21,000		
(G)	16,800		
ending bal.	15,300		

Work-in-Process Inventory Subsidiary Ledger

Job 100		Job 101		Job 102	
6,200	13,600 (H)	(B) 10,000	31,600 (H)	(B) 4,500	
(B) 2,000		(C) 12,000		(C) 6,000	
(C) 3,000		(G) 9,600		(G) 4,800	
(G) 2,400					
0		0		15,300	

Finished Goods Inventory			
beginning bal. 21,000	35,500	(I)	
(H)	45,200		
ending bal.	30,700		

Finished Goods Inventory Subsidiary Ledger

Job 99		Job 100		Job 101	
21,900	21,900 (I)	(H) 13,600	13,600 (I)	(H) 31,600	

Cost of Goods Sold	
(I)	35,500

Cost of Goods Sold Subsidiary Ledger

Job 99	Job 100
(I) 21,900	(I) 13,600

The letters in the T-accounts are the same as the code letters used in Figure 9-4.

Figure 9-5

The journal entries that follow support the transactions in Figure 9-5.

Job Order Cost System Journal Entries
General Journal

Date	Account Title and Description	Ref.	Debit	Credit
20X0				
Dec. 31	Raw Materials Inventory		15,000	
(A)	Accounts Payable			15,000
	Purchased raw materials on credit			
(B)	Work-in-Process Inventory		16,500	
	Raw Materials Inventory			16,500
	Raw materials used in jobs 100–102			
(C)	Work-in-Process Inventory		21,000	
	Wages Payable			21,000
	Direct labor incurred jobs 100–102			
(D)	Factory Overhead-Indirect Materials		5,700	
	Raw Materials Inventory			5,700
	Indirect materials requisitioned			

Date	Account Title and Description	Ref.	Debit	Credit
(E)	Factory Overhead-Indirect Labor		10,000	
	Wages Payable			10,000
	Indirect labor incurred			
(F)	Factory Overhead-Factory Rent*		1,200	
	Factory Overhead-Factory Utilities*		2,500	
	Accounts Payable			3,700
	Overhead costs incurred			
(G)	Work-in-Process Inventory		16,800	
	Factory Overhead			16,800
	Applied overhead for jobs 100–102			
(H)	Finished Goods Inventory		45,200	
	Work-in-Process Inventory			45,200
	Transfer completed jobs 100 & 101			
(I)	Cost of Goods Sold		35,500	
	Finished Goods Inventory			35,500
	**Transfer delivered jobs 99 & 100			

*   These are only example overhead accounts.

** Excludes portion of entry to recognize revenue on sale.

Process Cost System

Some companies have homogeneous or very similar products that are not made to order and are produced in large volumes. They continually process their product, moving it from one function to the next until it is completed. In these companies, the manufacturing costs incurred are allocated to the proper functions or departments within the factory process rather than to specific products. Examples of products that companies produce continuously are cereal, bread, candy, steel, automotive parts, chips, and computers. Companies that refine oil or bottle drinks and companies that provide services such as mail sorting and catalog order are also examples of continuous, homogeneous processing.

To illustrate, assume the Best Chips company manufactures potato chips. The company has three work areas they call preparation, baking, and packaging. The preparation area includes cutting potatoes and adding flavorings. Conveyor belts are used to move the product from one function to the next. In this company, raw materials are added in two of the functions: the preparation function and the packaging function. Labor and overhead are incurred in each function. Figure 9-6 shows the process flow and costs associated with Best Chip's process cost system.

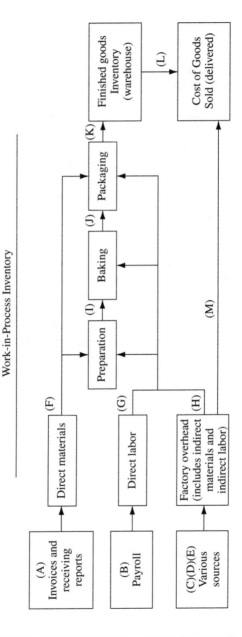

PROCESS COST SYSTEM COST FLOWS

Work-in-Process Inventory

Figure 9-6

The cost report for Best Chips summarizes how manufacturing costs (direct materials, direct labor, and manufacturing overhead) are assigned to the three departments. The report for June is as follows:

Best Chips
Cost Summary
For the Month Ended June 30, 20X2

	Raw Materials Inventory	Factory Labor	Factory Overhead	Work-in-Process Inventory		
				Preparation	Baking	Packaging
Beginning balance	5,200			3,200		
June costs	4,600	7,100	2,300			
Costs assigned						
Direct materials	(6,500)			2,800		3,700
Indirect materials	(1,300)		1,300			
Direct labor		(5,300)		2,900	500	
Indirect labor		(1,800)	1,800			
Factory overhead			(5,525)	435	3,000	2,090
Predetermined overhead rates				15%	600%	110%

The raw materials are assigned based on material requisition forms, the labor based on time tickets, and the overhead based on pre-determined overhead rates based on direct labor dollars. The journal entries to record these transactions are made prior to the period end entries that transfer the amounts from one work-in-process inventory account to another, from work-in-process inventory to finished goods inventory, and from finished goods inventory to cost of goods sold. The letters of the journal entries used to illustrate the accounting for process cost systems (see Key to Figure 9-4) correspond to the letters in Figure 9-6.

Raw materials requisitioned

Best Chips started the month of June with $5,200 in raw materials inventory. Best Chips uses the perpetual inventory method (see Chapter 8), so raw materials purchased are added to the raw material inventory account when they are received. Raw materials requisitioned that become part of the final product or are used by a specific function are considered direct materials used. The costs of direct materials are added to the proper department's work-in-process inventory account. Raw materials requisitioned that are used for general production purposes are added to factory overhead. The journal entries related to raw material activity for June are:

General Journal

Date	Account Title and Description	Ref.	Debit	Credit
20X2				
June 30	Raw Materials Inventory		4,600	
(A)	Accounts Payable			4,600
	Purchased raw materials on credit			

Date	Account Title and Description	Ref.	Debit	Credit
(C)	Factory Overhead		1,300	
	Raw Materials Inventory			1,300
	Indirect materials for June			
(F)	Work-in-Process Inventory-Preparation		2,800	
	Work-in-Process Inventory-Packaging		3,700	
	Raw Materials Inventory			6,500
	Transfer direct materials to work-in-process inventory			

At the end of the month, $2,000 of materials remained in raw materials inventory.

Raw Materials Inventory

beginning balance	5,200	1,300	(C)	
(A)	4,600	6,500	(F)	
	9,800	7,800		
ending balance	2,000			

Factory labor

As the factory labor payroll is prepared and recorded, the payroll costs are split between those employees who work in specific functions (departments) and those involved in the general functions of the factory. The specific function costs are called direct labor and are assigned to work-in-process inventory. The general factory labor costs are indirect labor costs that are added to factory overhead.

Unlike the accounting for payroll under the job order cost system, the employee does not have to be physically involved in making a product to be assigned to a specific function. If a specific maintenance worker or supervisor is assigned to the preparation function, their wages are allocated to that function even though these workers are not directly involved in preparing the chips to be baked. The accounting for the labor costs for June includes the following journal entries, shown in the following table.

General Journal

Date	Account Title and Description	Ref.	Debit	Credit
20X2				
June 30	Factory Labor		7,100	
(B)*	Wages Payable			7,100
	Record payroll for June			
(D)	Factory Overhead		1,800	
	Factory Labor			1,800
	Indirect labor for June			
(G)	Work-in-Process Inventory-Preparation		2,900	
	Work-in-Process Inventory-Baking		500	
	Work-in-Process Inventory-Packaging		1,900	
	Factory Labor			5,300
	Direct labor for June			

* This entry ignores the required withholdings for simplicity.

The balance in the factory labor account should be zero at the end of each period.

Factory Labor

(B)	7,100	1,800	(D)
		5,300	(G)
	7,100	7,100	
	0		

Factory overhead

In a process company, factory overhead represents those costs not directly assigned to one function. For example, the depreciation expense of a machine used solely by the preparation function would be assigned to work-in-process inventory for the preparation department while depreciation expense for the plant (the factory building) would be assigned to factory overhead as all functions occupy the plant. The journal entries that follow illustrate the accounting for general overhead costs.

General Journal

Date	Account Title and Description	Ref.	Debit	Credit
20X2				
June 30	Factory Overhead		2,300	
(E)	Prepaid Insurance			1,000
	Accounts Payable-Electric Utilities			1,200
	Cash			100
	June overhead x costs			

Date	Account Title and Description	Ref.	Debit	Credit
(H)	Work-in-Process Inventory-Preparation		435	
	Work-in-Process Inventory-Baking		3,000	
	Work-in-Process Inventory-Packaging		2,090	
	Factory Overhead			5,525
	Overhead allocated based on predetermined rates			

At the end of the period, the factory overhead account has a credit balance of ($125). This is called overapplied overhead and an entry would be made at the end of the period to move it to cost of goods sold, or alternatively, to allocate the difference to work-in-process inventories, finished goods inventory, and cost of goods sold. After recording this entry, the balance in the factory overhead account is zero.

General Journal

Date	Account Title and Description	Ref.	Debit	Credit
20X2				
June 30	Factory Overhead		125	
(M)	Cost of Goods Sold			125
	Close out overapplied overhead			

Work-in-process accounting

At the end of the period, entries are needed to record the cost of the products moved from one function (department) to another. In this example, costs are moved from work-in-process inventory-preparation to work-in-process inventory-baking and from work-in-process inventory-baking to work-in-process inventory-packaging. This is how the entries would look:

General Journal

Date	Account Title and Description	Ref.	Debit	Credit
20X2				
June 30	Work-in-Process Inventory-Baking		XXX	
(I)	Work-in-Process Inventory-Preparation			XXX
	Transfer June costs to Baking			
(J)	Work-in-Process Inventory-Packaging		XXX	
	Work-in-Process Inventory-Baking			XXX
	Transfer June costs to Packaging			

When the packaging function (department) completes its work, the product is ready to be sold. The costs of the completed products are then transferred from work-in-process inventory-packaging to finished goods inventory. This transfer also requires a journal entry.

General Journal

Date	Account Title and Description	Ref.	Debit	Credit
20X2				
June 30	Finished Goods Inventory		XXX	
(K)	Work-in-Process Inventory-Packaging			XXX
	Transfer to finished goods inventory			

The amounts for these journal entries are calculated by multiplying the cost per unit times the number of units that moved from one function to the next. The number of units is determined separately for each function using the actual number of units completed and transferred out of the function adjusted for partially completed units that were not transferred. This calculated number of units used is called **equivalent units**. If there are no in-process units at the beginning or end of the period, the per unit cost is calculated by dividing the total costs assigned to a function (department) by the total number of units that were started and completed during the period. The total costs include materials, labor, and overhead.

$$\text{Per unit cost of function} = \frac{\text{Total costs for function in period}}{\text{Total units started and completed}}$$

If the function has work-in-process inventory at the beginning of the period, the number of equivalent units must be calculated. Equivalent units represent the number of units that could have been 100% completed during the period. For example, if two employees each work 20 hours a week, this is the equivalent of one full-time employee (one equivalent unit). On a production line, if one product is 40% complete and a second one is 60% complete, this is the equivalent of 100% complete for one unit (one equivalent unit). This number is needed to spread the costs of the function over all the units worked on during the period. For example, if a company started 1,000 units of product during the period and at the end of the period these were 40% completed, the equivalent units would be 400 (1,000 units × 40% complete). This calculation assumes that the materials, labor, and overhead are all added evenly throughout the time the units are in process in the function. In many companies, the materials are all added at the beginning of the process while the labor and overhead costs are incurred throughout the process. Labor and overhead are also called **conversion costs** because they "convert" the materials into a product. If materials, labor, and overhead are added at different times in the production process, two separate calculations of equivalent units are necessary, one for the materials and one for conversion costs.

Using the previous example of 1,000 units started during the period that were 40% completed, assume that in a particular function, all of the materials are added at the beginning of the process and the labor and overhead are added evenly throughout the process. The equivalent units for materials would be the number of units times the percent complete. In this example, all the materials are added at the beginning of the process so 100% of materials for this function are included in all the units at the end of the period. The equivalent units for materials are 1,000 (1,000 units × 100% complete for materials). The total materials costs are divided by 1,000 to calculate the materials cost per unit.

Unlike materials, more labor and overhead will be needed before these units are transferred to another function or to finished goods. The equivalent units for conversion costs (labor and overhead) are 400 (1,000 units started × 40% complete for labor and overhead). The total conversion costs are divided by 400 to calculate the conversion costs per unit. To calculate total cost per unit, the materials cost per unit is added to the conversion cost per unit.

When a company has units that are started and completed during a period and has an ending inventory of units in process, most often the weighted average method is used to calculate equivalent units. If needed, based on the company's production processes, separate calculations of equivalent units for materials and conversion costs are made. Assume a company has two functions in its production process called Department 1 and Department 2. For the month of January, Department 1 completed and transferred out 2,000 units to Department 2 and had 800 units in process at month end that were 80% completed as to materials, labor, and overhead. Using the weighted average method, equivalent units for Department 1 for January are 2,640 [(2,000 × 100%) + (800 × 80%)]. The beginning units and those started and completed are not separately identified in the calculation of equivalent units. When calculating the per unit cost using the weighted average method, the beginning work-in-process costs for the function are added to those costs incurred during the period and then divided by the equivalent units.

Equivalent units may also be calculated using the first-in, first-out (FIFO) method. Under the FIFO method of calculating equivalent units, the beginning units would be identified separately from those started and completed. Continuing with the previous example, if 700 units were in process and 40% completed at the beginning of January, during January Department 1 would have added the additional 60% of the costs necessary to complete the units. Using the FIFO method, the equivalent units for January would be 3,060, calculated as follows:

	Actual Units	% Completed during Month	Equivalent Units
Beginning units	700	60%	420
Started and completed	2,000	100%	2,000
Transferred out	2,700		2,420
Ending units	800	80%	640
Total	3,500		3,060

Process costing summary

Once the physical units have been identified and the equivalent units calculated, the per unit cost is calculated and the cost summary is prepared for each function. Assume the following facts and costs for Department 1 for August. Overhead costs are based on direct labor hours.

	Units Total	%Completed Materials	%Completed Conversion Costs
Beginning inventory	3,000	100%	60%
Started and completed	5,000	100%	100%
Ending	2,000	100%	30%
Total	10,000		

	Total	Materials	Conversion Costs
Beginning inventory	$ 5,010	$2,760	$ 2,250
Incurred in August			
Direct materials	5,740	5,740	
Direct labor	5,100		5,100
Overhead	3,400		3,400
Total Costs	$19,250	$8,500	$10,750

Figures 9-7 and 9-8 show the **process cost summary** for Department 1 using the previous information for August under the weighted average and FIFO methods, respectively. The summary includes sections for the flow of the units, equivalent units, unit costs for the period, costs to be allocated (costs to be accounted for), and allocation of costs to the units transferred out and those units in process at the end of the period (costs accounted for).

In the weighted average example (see Figure 9-7), the calculation of number of units accounted for does not differentiate between units in beginning inventory and those units started and completed during the period because the costs are averaged for all these units. The per unit costs are based on the equivalent units completed and the total costs incurred on those units. Under the FIFO method (see Figure 9-8), costs are tracked based on specific units. Per unit costs are current period unit costs and calculated based on equivalent units completed and costs incurred for the current period. For the units in the beginning inventory, once the current period costs are calculated, they are added to the costs incurred in prior periods to determine the total costs for these units.

DEPARTMENT 1 COST SUMMARY
WEIGHTED AVERAGE METHOD
FOR THE MONTH OF AUGUST 20X0

	Physical Units		
Units to account for			
Beginning work-in-process inventory	3,000		
Started during period	7,000		
Total units to account for	10,000		

		Equivalent Units	
Units accounted for		Materials	Conversion Costs
Transferred out	8,000	8,000	8,000
Ending work-in-process inventory	2,000	2,000	600
Total units accounted for	10,000	10,000	8,600

	Total		
Units cost calculations			
Total costs (1)	$19,250	$ 8,500	$10,750
Equivalent units (2)		10,000	8,600
Unit costs (1) / (2)	$ 2.10	$ 0.85	$ 1.25

Costs to account for			
Beginning work-in-process inventory	$ 5,010		
Incurred during period	14,240		
Total costs to account for	$19,250		

		Total	
Costs accounted for			
Transferred out (8,000 × $2.10)		$16,800	
Ending work-in-process inventory			
Materials (2,000 × $0.85)	$ 1,700		
Conversion costs (600 × $1.25)	750	2,450	
Total costs accounted for		$19,250	

Figure 9-7

DEPARTMENT 1 COST SUMMARY
FIFO METHOD
FOR THE MONTH OF AUGUST 20X0

	Physical Units	Materials	Conversion Costs
Units to account for			
Beginning work-in-process inventory	3,000		
Started during period	7,000		
Total units to account for	10,000		
		Equivalent Units	
		Materials	Conversion Costs
Units accounted for			
Beginning work-in-process inventory	3,000	0	1,200
Started and completed	5,000	5,000	5,000
Ending work-in-process inventory	2,000	2,000	600
Total units accounted for	10,000	7,000	6,800
Units cost calculations			
Total costs (1)		$ 5,740	$8,500
Equivalent units (2)		7,000	6,800
Unit costs (1) / (2)	$ 2.07	$ 0.82	$ 1.25

Costs to account for	
Direct materials	$ 5,740
Direct labor	5,100
Manufacturing overhead	3,400
Costs for period	14,240
Beginning work-in-process inventory	5,010
Total costs to account for	$19,250

Costs accounted for		
Work-in-process beginning of month		
Beginning costs		$ 5,010
Direct materials		0
Conversion costs (1,200 × $1.25)		1,500
Total costs to process beginning units		6,510
Started and completed (5,000 × $2.07)		10,350
Total costs transferred out		16,860
Ending work-in-process inventory		
Materials (2,000 × $0.82)	$ 1,640	
Conversion costs (600 × $1.25)	750	
Total cost ending work-in-process inventory		2,390
Total costs accounted for		$19,250

Figure 9-8

Traditionally, in a job order cost system and process cost system (see Chapter 9), overhead is allocated to a job or function based on direct labor hours, machine hours, or direct labor dollars. However, in some companies, new technologies have changed the manufacturing environment such that the number of hours worked or dollars earned by employees are no longer good indicators of how much overhead will be needed to complete a job or process products through a particular function. In such companies, activity-based costing (ABC) is used to allocate overhead costs to jobs or functions.

Activity-Based Costing Activities

Activity-based costing assumes that the steps or activities that must be followed to manufacture a product are what determine the overhead costs incurred. Each overhead cost, whether variable or fixed, is assigned to a category of costs. These cost categories are called activity cost pools. **Cost drivers** are the actual activities that cause the total cost in an activity cost pool to increase. The number of times materials are ordered, the number of production lines in a factory, and the number of shipments made to customers are all examples of activities that impact the costs a company incurs. When using ABC, the total cost of each activity pool is divided by the total number of units of the activity to determine the cost per unit.

$$\text{Activity-Based Cost per Unit} = \frac{\text{Total Activity Cost}}{\text{Total Number of Units for Activity}}$$

The number of activities a company has may be small, say five or six, or number in the hundreds. Computers make using ABC easier. Assume Lady Trekkers, Inc., has identified its activity cost pools and cost drivers (see the following table).

Activity Cost Pools	*Activity Cost Drivers*
Purchasing Department	Number of Purchase Orders
Receiving Department	Number of Purchase Orders
Materials Handling	Number of Materials Requisitions
Setup	Number of Machine Setups Required
Inspection	Number of Inspections
Engineering Department	Number of Engineering Change Orders
Personnel Processing	Number of Employees Hired or Laid Off
Supervisors	Number of Direct Labor Hours

A per unit cost is calculated by dividing the total dollars in each activity cost pool by the number of units of the activity cost drivers. As an example to calculate the per unit cost for the purchasing department, the total costs of the purchasing department are divided by the number of purchase orders. Lady Trekkers, Inc., has determined that both the purchasing and receiving departments' costs are based on the number of purchase orders; therefore, the two departments' costs may be added together so that one per unit cost is calculated for these departments. Once the per unit costs are all calculated, they are added together, and the total cost per unit is multiplied by the number of units to assign the overhead costs to the units.

Activity categories

While using cost drivers to assign overhead costs to individual units works well for some activities, for some activities such as setup costs, the costs are not incurred to produce an individual unit but rather to produce a batch of the same units. For other costs, the costs incurred might be based on the number of product lines or simply because there is a manufacturing facility. To assign overhead costs more accurately, activity-based costing assigns activities to one of four categories:

- **Unit-level activities** occur every time a service is performed or a product is made. The costs of direct materials, direct labor, and machine maintenance are examples of unit-level activities.

- **Batch-level activities** are costs incurred every time a group (batch) of units is produced or a series of steps is performed. Purchase orders, machine setup, and quality tests are examples of batch-level activities.

- **Product-line activities** are those activities that support an entire product line but not necessarily each individual unit. Examples of product-line activities are engineering changes made in the assembly line, product design changes, and warehousing and storage costs for each product line.

- **Facility support activities** are necessary for development and production to take place. These costs are administrative in nature and include building depreciation, property taxes, plant security, insurance, accounting, outside landscape and maintenance, and plant management's and support staff's salaries.

The costs of unit-level, batch-level, and product-line activities are easily allocated to a specific product, either directly as a unit-level activity or through allocation of a pooled cost for batch-level and product-line activities. In contrast, the facility-level costs are kept separate from product costs and are not allocated to individual units because the allocation would have to be made on an arbitrary basis such as square feet, number of divisions or products, and so on.

Comparison of Activity-Based Costing and Traditional Cost System

Assume the Busy Ball Company makes two types of bouncing balls; one has a hollow center and the other has a solid center. The same equipment is used to produce the balls in different runs. Between batches, the equipment is cleaned, maintained, and set up in the proper configuration for the next batch. The hollow center balls are packaged with two balls per package, and the solid center balls are packaged one per package. During the year, Busy Ball expects to make 1,000,000 hollow center balls and 2,000,000 solid center balls. The overhead costs incurred have been allocated to activity pools as follows:

Purchasing of materials	$ 200,000
Setup of machines	350,280
Packaging	300,000
Testing	270,000
Cleaning and maintenance	288,540
Total overhead costs	$1,408,820

By analyzing the activity pools, the accountants and production managers have identified the cost drivers, estimated the total expected units for each product, and calculated the unit cost for each cost driver.

Activity	Cost Driver	Total Expected Units for Cost Driver (1)	Total Cost (2)	Unit Cost per Cost Driver (3) = (2) ÷ (1)
Purchasing of Materials	# purchase orders	100	$200,000	$2,000.00
Set up of Machines	# setups	252	350,280	1,390.00
Packaging	# containers filled	2,500,000	300,000	0.12
Testing	# tests	3,000	270,000	90.00
Cleaning and maintenance	# of runs	252	288,540	1,145.00

The activity by product is shown in the following table.

Activity	Cost Driver	Unit Cost (3)	Expected Use		ABC Cost Assigned	
			Hollow Center (4)	Solid Center (5)	Hollow Center (3) × (4)	Solid Center (3) × (5)
Purchasing	# purchase orders	$2,000.00	50	50	$100,000	$100,000
Setup	# setups	1,390.00	126	126	175,140	175,140
Packaging	# containers filled	0.12	500,000	2,000,000	60,000	240,000
Testing	# tests	90.00	1,000	2,000	90,000	180,000
Cleaning and maintenance	# runs	1,145.00	84	168	96,180	192,360
Totals					$521,320	$887,500

To calculate the per unit overhead costs under ABC, the costs assigned to each product are divided by the number of units produced. In this case, the unit cost for a hollow center ball is $0.52 and the unit cost for a solid center ball is $0.44.

$$\frac{\text{Overhead costs assigned to hollow center balls}}{\text{Number of hollow center balls}} = \frac{\$521,320}{1,000,000} = \$0.521$$

$$\frac{\text{Overhead costs assigned to solid center balls}}{\text{Number of solid center balls}} = \frac{\$887,500}{2,000,000} = \$0.444$$

Under the traditional method of allocating overhead based on direct labor dollars, the total costs for all balls would be divided by total direct labor dollars for all balls to determine the per unit cost. Estimated direct labor costs for the year are $1,512,000, of which $378,000 is for hollow center balls and $1,134,000 is for solid center balls. The per unit direct labor costs are $0.38 for hollow center balls ($378,000 ÷ 1,000,000) and $0.57 for solid center balls ($1,134,000 ÷ 2,000,000). The per unit cost to produce balls is calculated in two steps:

1. Calculate the predetermined overhead rate by dividing total overhead costs by total direct labor dollars.

2. Allocate overhead to each type of product by multiplying the overhead cost per direct labor dollar by the per unit direct labor dollars for hollow center balls and for solid center balls.

Step 1: Calculate overhead per direct labor dollar

$$\frac{\text{Total overhead costs}}{\text{Total direct labor dollars}} = \frac{\$1,408,820}{\$1,512,000} = \$0.932 \text{ per direct labor dollar}$$

Step 2: Allocation of overhead

Overhead cost per direct labor dollar × Per unit direct labor dollars

Hollow center balls
$0.932 × $0.378 = $0.352 overhead per unit

Solid center balls
$0.932 × $0.567 = $0.528 overhead per unit

A comparison of the overhead per unit calculated using the ABC and traditional methods often shows very different results:

Busy Ball Company
20X0 Overhead per Unit

	ABC	*Traditional*
Hollow Center Ball	$0.52	$0.35
Solid Center Ball	$0.44	$0.53

In this example, the overhead charged to the hollow ball using ABC is $0.52 and much higher than the $0.35 calculated under the traditional method. The $0.52 is a more accurate cost for making decisions about pricing and production. For the solid center ball, the overhead calculated is $0.44 per unit using the ABC method and $0.53 per unit using the traditional method. The reason for the differences is the traditional method determines the cost allocation using direct labor dollars only, so a product with high direct labor dollars gets allocated more of the overhead costs than a product with low direct labor dollars. The number of orders, setups, or tests the product actually uses does not impact the allocation of overhead costs when direct labor dollars are used to allocate overhead.

ABC provides a way to allocate costs more accurately when overhead costs are not incurred at the same rate as direct labor dollars. The more activities identified, the more complex the costing system becomes. Computer systems are needed for complex ABC systems. Some companies limit the number of activities used in the costing system to keep the system manageable. While this approach may result in some allocations being arbitrary, using ABC does provide a more accurate estimate of costs for use in making management decisions.

Management decisions, including those related to product costing, introduction of new products, or entry in a new market, require an understanding of how changes in revenues and costs impact profit. Fundamental to this understanding is learning about cost behavior.

Cost Behavior

The way a specific cost reacts to changes in activity levels is called **cost behavior**. Costs may stay the same or may change proportionately in response to a change in activity. Knowing how a cost reacts to a change in the level of activity makes it easier to create a budget, prepare a forecast, determine how much profit a new product will generate, and determine which of two alternatives should be selected.

Fixed costs

Fixed costs are those that stay the same in total regardless of the number of units produced or sold. Although total fixed costs are the same, fixed costs per unit changes as fewer or more units are produced. Straight-line depreciation is an example of a fixed cost. It does not matter whether the machine is used to produce 1,000 units or 10,000,000 units in a month, the depreciation expense is the same because it is based on the number of years the machine will be in service.

Variable costs

Variable costs are the costs that change in total each time an additional unit is produced or sold. With a variable cost, the per unit cost stays the same, but the more units produced or sold, the higher the total cost. Direct materials is a variable cost. If it takes one yard of fabric at a cost of $5 per yard to make one chair, the total materials cost for one chair is $5. The total cost for 10 chairs is $50 (10 chairs × $5 per chair) and the total cost for 100 chairs is $500 (100 chairs × $5 per chair).

Graphically, the total fixed cost looks like a straight horizontal line while the total variable cost line slopes upward.

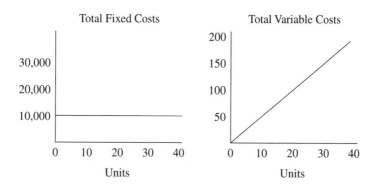

The graphs for the fixed cost per unit and variable cost per unit look exactly opposite the total fixed costs and total variable costs graphs. Although total fixed costs are constant, the fixed cost per unit changes with the number of units. The variable cost per unit is constant.

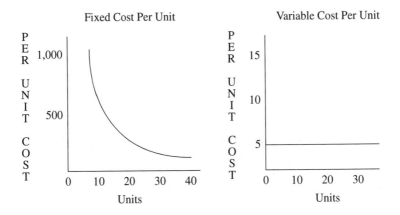

Fixed Cost Per Unit   Variable Cost Per Unit

When cost behavior is discussed, an assumption must be made about operating levels. At certain levels of activity, new machines might be needed, which results in more depreciation, or overtime may be required of existing employees, resulting in higher per hour direct labor costs. The definitions of fixed cost and variable cost assumes the company is operating or selling within the relevant range (the shaded area in the graphs) so additional costs will not be incurred.

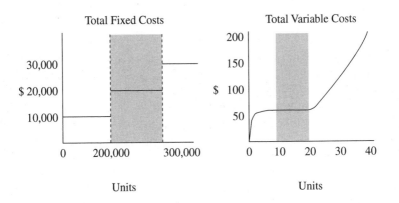

Total Fixed Costs   Total Variable Costs

Mixed costs

Some costs, called **mixed costs**, have characteristics of both fixed and variable costs. For example, a company pays a fee of $1,000 for the first 800 local phone calls in a month and $0.10 per local call made above 800. During March, a company made 2,000 local calls. Its phone bill will be $1,120 ($1,000 + (1,200 × $0.10)).

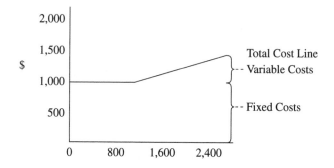

To analyze cost behavior when costs are mixed, the cost must be split into its fixed and variable components. Several methods, including scatter diagrams, the high-low method, and least-square regression, are used to identify the variable and fixed portions of a mixed cost, which are based on the past experience of the company.

Scatter diagram. In a **scatter diagram**, all parts would be plotted on a graph with activity (gallons of water used, in the example graph later in this section) on the horizontal axis and cost on the vertical axis. A line is drawn through the points and an estimate made for total fixed costs at the point where the line intersects the vertical axis at zero units of activity. To compute the variable cost per unit, the slope of the line is determined by choosing two points and dividing the change in their cost by the change in the units of activity for the two points selected.

For example, using data from the following example, if 36,000 gallons of water and 60,000 gallons of water were selected, the change in cost is $6,000 ($20,000 – $14,000) and the change in activity is 24,000 (60,000 – 36,000). This makes the slope of the line, the variable cost, $0.25 ($6,000 ÷ 24,000), and the fixed costs $5,000. See the graph to illustrate the point.

	Gallons of Water Used	Total Cost
January	50,000	$17,500
February	75,000	20,000
March	36,000	14,000
April	32,000	13,000
May	60,000	20,000
June	67,000	21,750

High-low method. The **high-low method** divides the change in costs for the highest and lowest levels of activity by the change in units for the highest and lowest levels of activity to estimate variable costs. The high point of activity is 75,000 gallons and the low point is 32,000 gallons. The variable cost per unit is estimated to be $0.163. It was calculated by dividing $7,000 ($20,000 − $13,000) by 43,000 (75,000 − 32,000) gallons of water.

Least-squares regression analysis. The **least-squares regression** analysis is a statistical method used to calculate variable costs. It requires a computer spreadsheet program (for example, Excel) or calculator and uses all points of data instead of just two points like the high-low method.

Cost-Volume-Profit Analysis

Cost-volume-profit (CVP) analysis is used to determine how changes in costs and volume affect a company's operating income and net income. In performing this analysis, there are several assumptions made, including:

- Sales price per unit is constant.

- Variable costs per unit are constant.

- Total fixed costs are constant.

- Everything produced is sold.

- Costs are only affected because activity changes.

- If a company sells more than one product, they are sold in the same mix.

CVP analysis requires that all the company's costs, including manufacturing, selling, and administrative costs, be identified as variable or fixed.

Contribution margin and contribution margin ratio

Key calculations when using CVP analysis are the **contribution margin** and the **contribution margin ratio**. The contribution margin represents the amount of income or profit the company made before deducting its fixed costs. Said another way, it is the amount of sales dollars available to cover (or contribute to) fixed costs. When calculated as a ratio, it is the percent of sales dollars available to cover fixed costs. Once fixed costs are covered, the next dollar of sales results in the company having income.

The contribution margin is sales revenue minus all variable costs. It may be calculated using dollars or on a per unit basis. If The Three M's, Inc., has sales of $750,000 and total variable costs of $450,000, its contribution margin is $300,000. Assuming the company sold 250,000 units during the year, the per unit sales price is $3 and the total variable cost per unit is $1.80. The contribution margin per unit is $1.20. The contribution margin ratio is 40%. It can be calculated using either the contribution margin in dollars or the contribution margin per unit. To calculate the contribution margin ratio, the contribution margin is divided by the sales or revenues amount.

Contribution Margin

	$	Per unit
Sales	$750,000	$3.00
Variable Costs	450,000	1.80
Contribution Margin	300,000	$1.20

Contribution Margin Ratio

$$\frac{\text{Contribution Margin}}{\text{Sales}} = \frac{\$300,000}{\$750,000} = 40\% \qquad \frac{\$1.20}{\$3.00} = 40\%$$

Break-even point

The break-even point represents the level of sales where net income equals zero. In other words, the point where sales revenue equals total variable costs plus total fixed costs, and contribution margin equals fixed costs. Using the previous information and given that the company has fixed costs of $300,000, the break-even income statement shows zero net income.

The Three M's, Inc.
Break-Even Income Statement

Revenues (250,000 units × $3)	$750,000
Variable Costs (250,000 units × $1.80)	450,000
Contribution Margin	300,000
Fixed Costs	300,000
Net Income	$ 0

This income statement format is known as the **contribution margin income statement** and is used for internal reporting only.

The $1.80 per unit or $450,000 of variable costs represent all variable costs including costs classified as manufacturing costs, selling expenses, and administrative expenses. Similarly, the fixed costs represent total manufacturing, selling, and administrative fixed costs.

Break-even point in dollars. The break-even point in sales dollars of $750,000 is calculated by dividing total fixed costs of $300,000 by the contribution margin ratio of 40%.

$$\frac{\text{Break-Even}}{\text{Sales Dollars}} = \frac{\text{Total Fixed Costs}}{\text{Contribution Margin Ratio}} = \frac{\$300,000}{40\%} = \$750,000$$

Another way to calculate break-even sales dollars is to use the mathematical equation.

Break-even Sales Dollars = Variable Costs + Fixed Costs

In this equation, the variable costs are stated as a percent of sales. If a unit has a $3.00 selling price and variable costs of $1.80, variable costs as a percent of sales is 60% ($1.80 ÷ $3.00). Using fixed costs of $300,000, the break-even equation is shown below.

Break-even Sales Dollars = Variable Costs + Fixed Costs

$$OR \quad \begin{array}{l} X = 60\% \; X + \$300,000 \\ X = .6X + \$300,000 \\ .4X = \$300,000 \\ X = \dfrac{\$300,000}{.4} \\ X = \$750,000 \text{ Break-even Sales} \end{array}$$

The last calculation using the mathematical equation is the same as the break-even sales formula using the fixed costs and the contribution margin ratio previously discussed in this chapter.

Break-even point in units. The break-even point in units of 250,000 is calculated by dividing fixed costs of $300,000 by contribution margin per unit of $1.20.

$$\text{Break-even Sales Units} = \frac{\text{Total Fixed Costs}}{\text{Contribution Margin Per Unit}} = \frac{\$300,000}{\$1.20} = 250,000 \text{ units}$$

The break-even point in units may also be calculated using the mathematical equation where "X" equals break-even units.

Break-even Sales Units

Sales = Variable Costs + Fixed Costs

$$\$3.00X = \$1.80X + \$300{,}000$$
$$\$1.20X = \$300{,}000$$
$$X = \frac{\$300{,}000}{\$1.20}$$

$$X = 250{,}000 \text{ Break-even Units}$$

Again it should be noted that the last portion of the calculation using the mathematical equation is the same as the first calculation of break-even units that used the contribution margin per unit. Once the break-even point in units has been calculated, the break-even point in sales dollars may be calculated by multiplying the number of break-even units by the selling price per unit. This also works in reverse. If the break-even point in sales dollars is known, it can be divided by the selling price per unit to determine the break-even point in units.

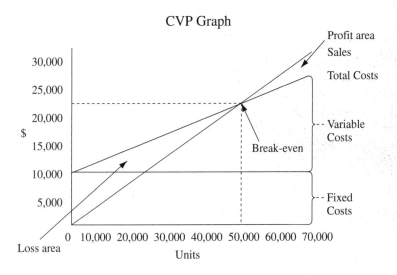

CVP Graph

Targeted income

CVP analysis is also used when a company is trying to determine what level of sales is necessary to reach a specific level of income, also called **targeted income**. To calculate the required sales level, the targeted income is added to fixed costs, and the total is divided by the contribution margin ratio to determine required sales dollars, or the total is divided by contribution margin per unit to determine the required sales level in units.

$$\text{Required Sales in Dollars} = \frac{\text{Fixed Costs} + \text{Targeted Income}}{\text{Contribution Margin Ratio}}$$

$$\text{Required Sales in Units} = \frac{\text{Fixed Costs} + \text{Targeted Income}}{\text{Contribution Margin Per Unit}}$$

Using the data from the previous example, what level of sales would be required if the company wanted $60,000 of income? The $60,000 of income required is called the targeted income. The required sales level is $900,000 and the required number of units is 300,000. Why is the answer $900,000 instead of $810,000 ($750,000 [break-even sales] plus $60,000)? Remember that there are additional variable costs incurred every time an additional unit is sold, and these costs reduce the extra revenues when calculating income.

$$\text{Required Sales in Dollars} = \frac{\$300,000 + \$60,000}{40\%} = \$900,000$$

$$\text{Required Sales in Units} = \frac{\$300,000 + \$60,000}{\$1.20} = 300,000 \text{ units}$$

This calculation of targeted income assumes it is being calculated for a division as it ignores income taxes. If a targeted net income (income after taxes) is being calculated, then income taxes would also be added to fixed costs along with targeted net income.

$$\text{Required Sales in Dollars} = \frac{\text{Fixed Costs + Targeted Income + Income Taxes}}{\text{Contribution Margin Ratio}}$$

$$\text{Required Sales in Units} = \frac{\text{Fixed Costs + Targeted Income + Income Taxes}}{\text{Contribution Margin Per Unit}}$$

Assuming the company has a 40% income tax rate, its break-even point in sales is $1,000,000 and break-even point in units is 333,333. The amount of income taxes used in the calculation is $40,000 ([$60,000 net income ÷ (1 − .40 tax rate)] − $60,000).

$$\text{Required Sales in Dollars} = \frac{\$300,000 + \$60,000 + \$40,000}{40\%} = \$1,000,000$$

$$\text{Required Sales in Units} = \frac{\$300,000 + \$60,000 + \$40,000}{\$1.20} = 333,333 \text{ units}$$

A summarized contribution margin income statement can be used to prove these calculations.

The Three M's, Inc.
Income Statement
20X0 Targeted Net Income

Sales (333,333* units × $3)	$1,000,000
Variable Costs (333,333* units × $1.80)	600,000
Contribution Margin	400,000
Fixed Costs	300,000
Income before Taxes	100,000
Income Taxes (40%)	40,000
Net Income	$ 60,000

* Rounded

Margin of Safety

The **margin of safety** is a tool to help management understand how far sales could change before the company would have a net loss. It is computed by subtracting break-even sales from budgeted or forecasted sales. To state the margin of safety as a percent, the difference is divided by budgeted sales. If the Three M's, Inc., has budgeted sales of $800,000, its margin of safety is $50,000 ($800,000 budgeted sales − $750,000 break-even sales) or 6.7% ($50,000 ÷ $750,000), a rather low margin of safety. If, however, its budgeted sales are $900,000, its margin of safety is $150,000 ($900,000 budgeted sales − $750,000 break-even sales) or 20% ($150,000 ÷ $750,000). The competition, economy, and assumptions in the sales budget must be reviewed by management to assess whether 20% is a comfortable margin of safety.

Sensitivity Analysis

A business environment can change quickly, so a business should understand how sensitive its sales, costs, and income are to changes. CVP analysis using the break-even formula is often used for this analysis. For example, marketing suggests a higher quality product would allow The Three M's, Inc., to raise its selling price 10%, from $3.00 to $3.30. To increase the quality would increase variable costs to $2.00 per unit and fixed costs to $350,000. If The Three M's, Inc., followed this scenario, its break-even in units would be 269,231.

$$\frac{\text{Break-even}}{\text{Sales Units}} = \frac{\text{Total Fixed Costs}}{\text{Contribution Margin Per Unit}} = \frac{\$350,000}{\$1.30^*} = 269,231 \text{ units}$$

* $3.30 selling price − $2.00 variable costs

These changes in variable costs and sales result in a higher break-even point in units than the 250,000 break-even units calculated with the original assumptions. The critical question is, "Will the customers continue to purchase, and are new or existing customers identified that will purchase the additional 19,231 units of the product required to break even at the higher sales price?"

Budgets are part of a company's long-range planning system. While some portions of a long-range plan are concerned with the organization in five to ten years, the **budget** is the short-range portion of the plan. Most budgets are prepared for a twelve-month period, sometimes on a rolling basis. A **rolling budget** is updated quarterly (or as often as management requires the data) by dropping the three months just ended and adding one quarter's data to the end of the remaining nine months already budgeted (see following figure). Rolling budgets require management to keep looking forward and to anticipate changes.

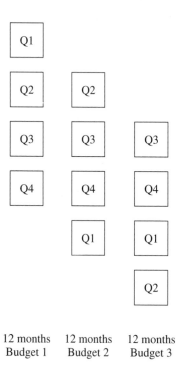

The **master budget** consists of all the individual budgets required to prepare budgeted financial statements. Although different textbooks group the budgets differently, the main components of a budget are operating budgets for revenues and expenses, capital expenditures budget, cash budget, and finally the budgeted financial statements, which include the income statement, balance sheet, and cash flow statement.

Operating Budgets

The operating budgets include the budgets for sales, manufacturing costs (materials, labor, and overhead) or merchandise purchases, selling expenses, and general and administrative expenses.

Sales budget

The **sales budget** is the starting point in putting together a comprehensive budget for a business. It includes the number of units to be sold and the selling price per unit. It is important to agree to the sales budget first because many other budgets are based on this data. Although its components are simple, getting a management team to agree on the number of units to be sold and the selling price per unit, the two items needed to prepare the budget, is often difficult and time-consuming. The Pickup Trucks Company, which makes toy trucks, has just completed its budgeting process for next year. Total expected sales are 100,000 toy trucks at a price of $15.00 each. Its sales budget has been prepared on a quarterly basis as follows:

The Pickup Trucks Company
Sales Budget
For the Year Ended December 31, 20X1

	Quarter 1	Quarter 2	Quarter 3	Quarter 4	Total
Units	15,000	17,000	28,000	40,000	100,000
Selling Price	$15	$15	$15	$15	$15
Total Sales	$225,000	$255,000	$420,000	$600,000	$1,500,000

In addition to annual and quarterly sales budgets, monthly budgets are often prepared so sales can be tracked against expectations more frequently than once every three months.

Manufacturing costs

Before preparing the direct materials, direct labor, and manufacturing overhead budgets, the production budget must be completed.

Production budget. The **production budget** shows the number of units that must be produced. To budget for annual production, three things must be known: the number of units to be sold, the required level of inventory at the end of the year, and the number of units, if any, in the beginning inventory. If quarterly budgets are required, this same information is needed on a quarterly basis. Using the Pickup Trucks Company's quarterly sales budget and given that 15% of the next quarter's sales volume must be on hand before the quarter begins, the production budget by quarter can be prepared. Further assumptions are a 10% increase in sales in quarter one of next year compared to the current year's quarter-one sales, and 2,250 units in inventory at the beginning of the year.

Pickup Trucks Company
Production Budget in Units
For 20X1

	Quarter 1	Quarter 2	Quarter 3	Quarter 4	Total
Sales	15,000	17,000	28,000	40,000	100,000
Required Ending Inventory (1)	2,550(2)	4,200(2)	6,000(2)	2,475(4)	2,475(5)
Units Required	17,550	21,200	34,000	42,475	102,475
Beginning Inventory	(2,250)(3)	(2,550)(2)	(4,200)(2)	(6,000)(2)	(2,250)(6)
Units to be Produced	15,300	18,650	29,800	36,475	100,225

Notes:

1. Required ending inventory equals 15% times the next quarter's sales. For quarter one that is 15% × 17,000 (quarter two's sales) = 2,550.

2. The end of one quarter is the same as the beginning of the next quarter. So the ending inventory for quarter one (March 31) is the same as the beginning inventory for quarter two (April 1); the ending inventory for quarter two is the beginning inventory for quarter three, and so on.

3. The beginning inventory for quarter one was given as 2,250, but given the company's requirement that inventory on hand at the end of a quarter be 15% of next quarter's sales, it can also be calculated as 15% times 15,000 (quarter one's sales).

4. The ending inventory for quarter four is also 15% of the next quarter's sales. To complete the calculation, quarter one's sales for the next year must first be forecast. In this budget, quarter one's sales are expected to be 16,500 units, a 10% increase over the 15,000 units in the current year's budget for quarter one. Once the number of units for quarter one's sales is determined, the ending inventory can be calculated as 15% × 16,500 units = 2,475 units.

5. The 2,475 ending inventory at the end of quarter four is also the end of the year inventory.

6. The 2,250 represents the inventory at the beginning of the year (see quarter one).

Direct materials budget. The **direct materials budget** determines the number of units of raw materials to be purchased. It uses the number of units to be produced from the production budget, the required level of ending inventory for raw materials, and the number of units in beginning inventory. Once the number of units to be purchased is determined, it is multiplied by the cost per unit to determine the budgeted amount for raw materials purchases. The Pickup Trucks Company requires 10% of next quarter's production requirement for raw materials to be in its ending inventory. For example, because it takes five tires to make the special toy pickup truck (four plus the spare tire mounted on the side), at a cost of $0.50 per tire, the raw materials purchases budget calculates 501,890 tires required at a cost of $250,945. The units in the production budget are adjusted for units in ending and beginning inventories, multiplied by five (number of tires per pick up) to determine total tires to be purchased and then multiplied by $0.50 to determine the cost of the tires needed. As a reminder, the production budget showed the following units for 20X1:

	Units
Quarter 1	15,300
Quarter 2	18,650
Quarter 3	29,800
Quarter 4	36,475
Total	100,225

Pickup Trucks Company
Raw Materials Budget
For the Year 20X1

	Quarter 1	Quarter 2	Quarter 3	Quarter 4	Total
Units to be produced (1)	15,300	18,650	29,800	36,475	100,225
Number of tires per unit (2)	× 5	× 5	× 5	× 5	× 5
	76,500	93,250	149,000	182,375	501,125
Required ending inventory (3)	9,325	14,900	18,238	8,415 (4)	8,415
Total units required	85,825	108,150	167,238	190,790	509,540
Beginning inventory (3) (5)	(7,650)	(9,325)	(14,900)	(18,238)	(7,650)
Units to purchase	78,175	98,825	152,338	172,552	501,890
Cost per unit (6)	× $0.15	× $0.15	× $0.15	× $0.15	× $0.15
Cost of raw materials purchases*	$11,726	$ 14,824	$ 22,851	$ 25,883	$ 75,284

* Rounded

Notes:

1. Units to be produced from the production budget.

2. Number of units of raw material for one unit produced.

3. Required ending inventory level is 10% of next quarter's raw materials' requirement. The ending inventory is also used as the beginning inventory for the following quarter.

4. The required inventory is 10% of quarter one's raw materials' requirement. Since quarter one's production is 16,830 units or 84,150 tires, 10% of 84,150 is 8,415 tires.

5. The beginning inventory is 10% of the next quarter's raw materials' requirement for production. For quarter one, the raw materials' requirement is 10% of 76,500.

6. Each tire costs $0.15.

This process is repeated for all the other raw material components used in producing a toy pickup truck.

Direct labor budget. The direct labor budget shows the number of direct labor hours and the cost of the labor to determine the total cost of direct labor. Assume it takes one-half hour of labor to put together one pickup truck and each labor hour costs $14.00. The total direct labor budget is for 50,113 (100,225 units × .5 hours per unit) hours at a cost of $701,575 ($14.00 per hour × 50,113 hours). The break out by quarter is shown in the following table.

Pickup Trucks Company
Direct Labor Budget
For the Year 20X1

	Quarter 1	Quarter 2	Quarter 3	Quarter 4	Total
Units to be produced	15,300	18,650	29,800	36,475	100,225
Direct labor hours per unit	× .5	× .5	× .5	× .5	× .5
Total direct labor hours	7,650	9,325	14,900	18,237.5	50,112.5
Cost per hour	× $14.00	× $14.00	× $14.00	× $14.00	× $14.00
Cost of direct labor	$107,100	$130,550	$208,600	$255,325	$701,575

Manufacturing overhead. The **manufacturing overhead budget** identifies the expected variable and fixed overhead costs for the year (or other period) being budgeted. The separation between fixed and variable costs is important because the Pickup Trucks Company uses a predetermined overhead rate for applying overhead to units produced. In preparing its budget, the Pickup Trucks Company has identified the following variable and fixed costs: indirect materials $0.50 per unit, indirect labor $1.00 per unit, maintenance $0.75 per unit, annual depreciation $12,000, supervisory salaries $24,000, and property taxes and insurance $21,000. The budget by quarter is:

Pickup Trucks Company
Manufacturing Overhead Budget
For the Year 20X1

	Quarter 1	Quarter 2	Quarter 3	Quarter 4	Total
Variable Costs					
Indirect Materials	$ 7,650	$ 9,325	$14,900	$18,238	$ 50,113
Indirect Labor	15,300	18,650	29,800	36,475	100,225
Maintenance	11,475	13,988	22,350	27,356	75,169
Total Variable Costs	34,425	41,963	67,050	82,069	225,507
Fixed Costs					
Supervisory Salaries	3,000	3,000	3,000	5,700	14,700
Property Taxes and Insurance	6,000	6,000	6,000	6,000	24,000
Depreciation	5,250	5,250	5,250	5,250	21,000
Total Fixed Costs	14,250	14,250	14,250	16,950	59,700
Total Manufacturing Overhead	$48,675	$56,213	$81,300	$99,019	$285,207
Total Direct Labor Hours*	7,650	9,325	14,900	18,238	50,113
Predetermined Overhead Rate					$5.70

* Rounded

Selling expenses budget

The budget for selling expenses includes the variable and fixed selling expenses. The variable expenses in the selling expenses budget are usually based on sales dollars. Assume the Pickup Trucks Company's variable expenses are sales commissions and delivery expense. Sales commissions are 4% of sales dollars, and delivery expense, also called *freight out* by some companies, is $0.10 per unit sold. The company also has fixed sales salaries of $50,000. The calculations for sales commissions and delivery expense, followed by the selling expenses budget, are shown in the following tables.

Pickup Trucks Company
Sales Commission and Delivery Expenses Budget Calculations
For the Year 20X1

	Quarter 1	Quarter 2	Quarter 3	Quarter 4	Total
Sales Commission Expense					
Sales	$225,000	$255,000	$420,000	$600,000	$1,500,000
Commission Rate	4%	4%	4%	4%	4%
Sales Commissions	$ 9,000	$ 10,200	$ 16,800	$ 24,000	$ 60,000
Delivery Expense					
Units Sold	15,000	17,000	28,000	40,000	100,000
Cost per Unit	$0.10	$0.10	$0.10	$0.10	$0.10
Delivery Expense	$ 1,500	$ 1,700	$ 2,800	$ 4,000	$10,000

Pickup Trucks Company
Selling Expenses Budget
For the Year 20X1

	Quarter 1	Quarter 2	Quarter 3	Quarter 4	Total
Variable Expenses					
Sales Commissions	$ 9,000	$10,200	$16,800	$24,000	$ 60,000
Delivery Expense	1,500	1,700	2,800	4,000	10,000
Total Variable Expenses	10,500	11,900	19,600	28,000	70,000
Fixed Expenses					
Sales Salaries	12,500	12,500	12,500	12,500	50,000
Total Selling Expenses	$23,000	$24,400	$32,100	$40,500	$120,000

General and administrative expenses budget

The **general and administrative expenses budget** details the variable and fixed operating expenses for the general and administrative areas of the company. The Pickup Trucks Company has no variable administrative expenses. Its fixed expenses include salaries of $60,000, rent expense of $15,000, and office supplies of $6,000.

Pickup Trucks Company
General and Administrative Expenses Budget
For the Year 20X1

	Quarter 1	*Quarter 2*	*Quarter 3*	*Quarter 4*	*Total*
Variable Expenses					
None					
Fixed Expenses					
Salaries	$15,000	$15,000	$15,000	$15,000	$60,000
Rent Expense	3,750	3,750	3,750	3,750	15,000
Office Supplies	1,500	1,500	1,500	1,500	6,000
Total General and Administrative Expenses	$20,250	$20,250	$20,250	$20,250	$81,000

Capital Expenditures Budget

The **capital expenditures budget** identifies the amount of cash a company will invest in projects and long-term assets. Although funds for expenditures may be identified and approved in total during the budget process, most companies have a separate process for approving funds for the specific items included in a capital expenditures budget. The process includes a financial evaluation to determine whether the company's return on investment targets are met and, once the targets are known to be met, a qualitative review by a top management team. Many companies include long-term assets, such as joint ventures, purchases of other companies, and purchases or leases of fixed assets, as well as new products, new markets, research and development, significant marketing programs, and information technology items in their capital expenditures budgets.

Cash Budget

The **cash budget** is prepared after the operating budgets (sales, manufacturing expenses or merchandise purchases, selling expenses, and general and administrative expenses) and the capital expenditures budget are prepared. The cash budget starts with the beginning cash balance to which is added the cash inflows to get cash available. Cash outflows for the period are then subtracted to calculate the cash balance before financing. If this balance is below the company's required balance, the financing section shows the borrowings needed. The financing section also includes debt repayments, including interest payments. The cash balance before financing is adjusted by the financing activity to calculate the ending cash balance. The ending cash balance is the cash balance in the budgeted or pro forma balance sheet.

In keeping with the budgets previously discussed for the Pickup Trucks Company, the cash budget in this example will be prepared on a quarterly basis. In addition to the information in the budgets previously prepared, the following information is needed to complete the cash budget.

1. The company is expected to end the current year with $20,000 cash, $162,000 in accounts receivable, and $24,862 in accounts payable.

2. The company's sales are all made on credit, with 70% of the balance collected in the quarter of the sale and 30% in the quarter after the sale.

3. The company plans to sell a piece of land in the third quarter for $15,000, its book value.

4. The total cost of raw materials to be purchased (including tires) are: $31,270 in quarter one; $39,530 in quarter two; $60,936 in quarter three; and $69,021 in quarter four.

5. Raw materials purchases are paid for 60% in the quarter of the purchase and 40% in the quarter after the purchase.

6. All other cash expenses are paid for in the quarter they are incurred.

7. Capital expenditures for 20X1 include the purchase of machines for $20,000 in quarter two and $56,000 in quarter three.

8. Income taxes for the current year are paid quarterly with the final payment being made in the first quarter of the following year.

9. The company requires a cash balance of $20,000 at the end of each quarter. Arrangements have been made with the bank to borrow if needed in even increments of $1,000. Assume all borrowings are made at the beginning of the quarter. Borrowings are paid back at the end of the next quarter with interest of 8%.

Before preparing the cash budget, the collections from customers and payments for raw materials purchases must be calculated.

Pickup Trucks Company
Collections from Customers
20X1

	Quarter 1	Quarter 2	Quarter 3	Quarter 4	Year
Beginning Balance ($162,000)	$162,000				$162,000
Quarter 1 Sales ($225,000) (1)	157,500	$ 67,500			225,000
Quarter 2 Sales ($255,000) (2)		178,500	$ 76,500		255,000
Quarter 3 Sales ($420,000) (3)			294,000	$126,000	420,000
Quarter 4 Sales ($600,000) (4)				420,000	420,000
Total Collections	$319,500	$246,000	$370,500	$546,000	$1,482,000

(1) Quarter 1 sales of $225,000 are collected 70% in quarter one and 30% in quarter two.
(2) Quarter 2 sales of $255,000 are collected 70% in quarter two and 30% in quarter three.
(3) Quarter 3 sales of $420,000 are collected 70% in quarter three and 30% in quarter four.
(4) Quarter 4 sales of $600,000 are collected 70% in quarter four and 30% in quarter one next year. This 30% is the balance in the accounts receivable account at the end of 20X1.

Pickup Trucks Company
Payments for Raw Materials
20X1

	Quarter 1	*Quarter 2*	*Quarter 3*	*Quarter 4*	*Year*
Beginning Balance ($24,862)	$24,862				$ 24,862
Quarter 1 Purchases ($31,270) (5)	18,762	$12,508			31,270
Quarter 2 Purchases ($39,530) (6)		23,718	$15,812		39,530
Quarter 3 Purchases ($60,936) (7)			36,562	$24,374	60,936
Quarter 4 Purchases ($69,021) (8)				41,413	41,413
Total Payments	$43,624	$36,226	$52,374	$65,787	$198,011

(5) Quarter 1 purchases of $31,270 are paid 60% in quarter one and 40% in quarter two.
(6) Quarter 2 purchases of $39,530 are paid 60% in quarter two and 40% in quarter three.
(7) Quarter 3 purchases of $60,936 are paid 60% in quarter three and 40% in quarter four.
(8) Quarter 4 purchases of $69,021 are paid 60% in quarter four and 40% in quarter one next year. This 40% is the balance in the accounts payable account at the end of 20X1.

Pickup Trucks Company
Cash Budget
For the Year 20X1

	#A	Quarter 1	Quarter 2	Quarter 3	Quarter 4	Year
Beginning Balance	1	$ 20,000	$ 85,351	$ 28,712	$ 20,588	$ 20,000
Cash Inflows						
Collections from Customers	2	319,500	246,000	370,500	546,000	1,482,000
Proceeds from land sale	3			15,000		15,000
Total Receipts		319,500	246,000	385,500	546,000	1,497,000
Cash Available		339,500	331,351	414,212	566,588	1,517,000
Cash Outflows						
Raw Materials Purchases	4,5	43,624	36,226	52,374	65,787	198,011
Direct Labor	6	107,100	130,550	208,600	255,325	701,575
Manufacturing Overhead (B)	6	45,675	53,213	78,300	93,319	270,507

	#	Quarter 1	Quarter 2	Quarter 3	Quarter 4	Year
Selling Expenses	6	23,000	24,400	32,100	40,500	120,000
Administrative Expenses	6	20,250	20,250	20,250	20,250	81,000
Purchases of Machinery	7		20,000	56,000		76,000
Income Taxes	8	14,500	18,000	18,000	18,000	68,500
Total Outflows		254,149	302,639	465,624	493,181	1,515,593
Cash Balance before financing		85,351	28,712	(51,412)	73,407	1,407
Financing						
Borrowings	9			72,000		72,000
Principal Repayments	9				(50,000)	(50,000)
Interest Payments	9				(2,880)	(2,880)
Net Borrowing Costs		0	0	72,000	(52,880)	19,120
Ending Cash Balance	9	$ 85,351	$ 28,712	$ 20,588	$ 20,527	$ 20,527

(A) The numbers refer to the additional information on page 16.

(B) Depreciation expense is not a cost outlay and is not included in the cash budget for manufacturing overhead.

Budgeted Income Statement

The budgeted or pro forma income statement is prepared after the operating budgets have been completed. The cost of goods sold on the income statement is calculated using the per unit cost of $11.25, which consists of $1.40 per unit for direct materials, $7.00 per unit for direct labor, and a manufacturing overhead rate of $2.85. The overhead rate is calculated by multiplying the predetermined overhead rate of $5.70 per direct labor hour times the direct labor hours per unit of one-half hour.

	Quantity	Unit Cost	Total Cost
Direct Materials	Various	$ 1.40	$ 1.40
Direct Labor	.5 hour	14.00	7.00
Manufacturing Overhead	.5 hour	5.70	2.85
Total Unit Cost			$11.25

Pickup Trucks Company
Budgeted Income Statement
For the Year 20X1

Sales (100,000 × $15)		$1,500,000
Cost of Goods Sold (100,000 × $11.25)		1,125,000
Gross Profit		375,000
Operating Expenses		
Selling Expenses	$120,000	
Administrative Expenses	81,000	
Total Operating Expenses		201,000
Income from Operations		174,000
Interest Expense		2,880
Income before Income Taxes		171,120
Income Taxes (40%)		68,448
Net Income		$ 102,672

Budgeted Balance Sheet

The **budgeted** or **pro forma balance sheet** projects the financial position of the company as of the end of the year. It is prepared by adjusting the beginning balances of long-term asset, liability, and stockholders' equity accounts for expected activity during the budgeted period, and identifying balances in current asset and liability accounts at the end of the period. The beginning balances for the long-term assets and stockholders' equity accounts are shown in the following table. The Pickup Trucks Company does not have any long-term liabilities.

Land	$ 45,000
Building	300,000
Equipment	60,000
Accumulated Depreciation	(50,000)
Common Stock	25,000
Additional Paid-in-Capital	350,000
Retained Earnings	89,799

Pickup Trucks Company
Budgeted Balance Sheet
20X1

Assets

Current Assets

Cash	$ 20,527
Accounts Receivable	180,000
Finished Goods Inventory	27,844
Raw Materials Inventory	2,356
Total Current Assets	230,727

Property, Plant and Equipment

Land	$ 30,000	
Building	300,000	
Equipment	136,000	
Less: Accumulated Depreciation	(65,200)	
Total Property, Plant and Equipment		400,800
Total Assets		$631,527

Liabilities and Stockholders' Equity

Current Liabilities

Notes Payable	$ 22,000
Accounts Payable	27,608
Income Taxes Payable	14,448
Total Current Liabilities	64,056

Stockholders' Equity

Common Stock, $1 par value, 1,000,000 shares authorized, 25,000 shares issued and outstanding	25,000
Additional Paid-in-Capital	350,000
Retained Earnings	192,471
Total Stockholders' Equity	567,471
Total Liabilities and Stockholders' Equity	$631,527

Explanations for each balance are as follows:

- **Cash:** Ending balance per the cash budget.

- **Accounts receivable:** 30% of fourth quarter sales ($600,000 × 30%).

- **Finished goods inventory:** 2,475 units (15% of next quarter's sales of 16,500) times $11.25 per unit cost. See production budget and cost of goods sold calculation for further information.

- **Raw materials inventory:** Materials for 1,683 units (10% of next quarter's production of 16,830 units) times $1.40 per unit cost of materials. See direct materials budget and cash budget for units and costs.

- **Land:** Sale of land with a cost of $15,000 (per cash budget information) deducted from beginning balance of $45,000.

- **Building:** No activity during the year.

- **Equipment:** Beginning balance of $60,000 plus purchases totaling $76,000.

- **Accumulated depreciation:** Beginning balance of $50,000 plus $15,200 additional depreciation per the manufacturing overhead budget.

- **Notes payable:** $72,000 in borrowings during the year minus $50,000 principal repayments per the cash budget.

- **Accounts payable:** 40% of fourth quarter purchases ($69,021 × 40%). See cash payments for raw materials in cash budget and its calculation spread sheet.

- **Income taxes payable:** Balance owed for current year taxes. Difference between estimated taxes paid (per cash budget for quarters two, three, and four) and the expense per budgeted income statement. The company did not make a payment of its 20X1 taxes in quarter one of 20X0; the payment in the cash budget quarter one is for 20X0 taxes.

- **Common stock:** No stock activity during the year.

- **Additional paid-in-capital:** No stock activity during the year.

- **Retained earnings:** Beginning balance $89,799 plus net income for the year of $102,672 per the budgeted income statement. Dividends were not declared and paid, and therefore none are deducted.

Merchandising Company Budgets

In a merchandising company, the production budget and the three manufacturing budgets—direct materials, direct labor, and manufacturing overhead—are replaced with the **merchandise purchases budget**. This budget is prepared using the same three components as the production budget—sales, required ending merchandise inventory, and beginning merchandise inventory. As with the production budget, the required ending inventory is added to the expected sales to determine total amount of merchandise needed, and beginning inventory is subtracted from the total to determine the amount of inventory that needs to be purchased. The number of units is multiplied by cost of the merchandise to complete the merchandise purchases budget. For example, assume The Sunny Beach T-Shirt Company plans to sell 25,000 T-shirts during quarter one, 10,000 during quarter two, 18,000 during quarter three, and 7,500 during quarter four. Given the timing of shipments, it maintains an inventory at the end of each quarter equal to 10% of the next quarter's sales. At a cost of $8 per T-shirt, the company's second quarter merchandise purchases budget is $86,400.

The Sunny Beach T-Shirt Company
Merchandise Purchases Budget
For the Second Quarter 20X0

Sales units	10,000
Required units in ending inventory (10% × 18,000)	1,800
Merchandise required	11,800
Less: units in beginning inventory (10% × 10,000)	(1,000)
Required merchandise purchases	10,800
Cost per unit	× $8
Cost of merchandise purchases	$86,400

The remaining budgets of a merchandising company (sales, selling expenses, general and administrative expenses, capital expenditures, cash, income statement, and balance sheet) are the same as those discussed for a manufacturing company.

FLEXIBLE BUDGETS

A **budget report** is prepared to show how actual results compare to the budgeted numbers. It has columns for the actual and budgeted amounts and the differences, or variances, between these amounts. A variance may be favorable or unfavorable. On an income statement budget report, think of how the variance affects net income, and you will know if it is a favorable or unfavorable variance. If the actual results cause net income to be higher than budgeted net income (such as more revenues than budgeted or lower than budgeted costs), the variance is favorable. If actual net income is lower than planned (lower revenues than planned and/or higher costs than planned), the variance is unfavorable. So higher revenues cause a favorable variance, while higher costs and expenses cause an unfavorable variance.

Although the budget report shows variances, it does not explain the reasons for the variance. The budget report is used by management to identify the sales or expenses whose amounts are not what were expected so management can find out why the variances occurred. By understanding the variances, management can decide whether any action is needed. Favorable variances are usually positive amounts, and unfavorable variances are usually negative amounts. Some textbooks show budget reports with "F" for favorable and "U" for unfavorable after the variances to further highlight the type of variance being reported.

Pick Up Trucks Company
Budget Report
For the Second Quarter 20X1

	Actual	Budget	Variance—Favorable/(Unfavorable)
Sales Units	17,500	17,000	
Sales	$259,000	$255,000	$ 4,000
Cost of Goods Sold	196,875	191,250	(5,625)
Gross Profit	62,125	63,750	(1,625)
Selling Expenses	24,610	24,400	(210)
General and Administrative Expenses	20,250	20,250	0
Operating Income	17,265	19,100	(1,835)
Interest Expense	0	0	0
Income before Income Taxes	17,265	19,100	(1,835)
Income Taxes	6,906	7,640	734
Net Income	$ 10,359	$ 11,460	($1,101)

Actual net income is unfavorable compared to the budget. What is not known from looking at it is why the variances occurred. For example, were more units sold? Was the selling price different than expected? Were costs higher? Or was it all of the above? These are the kinds of questions management needs answers to. In fact, an analysis of this budget report shows sales were actually 17,500 pickup trucks instead of the 17,000 pickup trucks planned; the average selling price was $14.80 per truck instead of the expected $15.00 per truck; and the cost per truck was $11.25 as budgeted.

Static budgets are geared to one level of activity. They work well for evaluating performance when the planned level of activity is the same as the actual level of activity, or when the budget report is prepared for fixed costs. However, if actual performance in a given month or quarter is different from the planned amount, it is difficult to determine whether costs were controlled.

Flexible budgets are one way companies deal with different levels of activity. A **flexible budget** provides budgeted data for different levels of activity. Another way of thinking of a flexible budget is a number of static budgets. For example, a restaurant may serve 100, 150, or 300 customers an evening. If a budget is prepared assuming 100 customers will be served, how will the managers be evaluated if 300 customers are served? Similar scenarios exist with merchandising and manufacturing companies. To effectively evaluate the restaurant's performance in controlling costs, management must use a budget prepared for the actual level of activity. This does not mean management ignores differences in sales level, or customers eating in a restaurant, because those differences and the management actions that caused them need to be evaluated, too.

The budget report for the Pickup Trucks Company (see Chapter 12) is a static budget because the budgeted level of units is the same number of units as the original budget. It was not changed for the higher sales level. If it had, the budget report would be as follows:

Pick Up Trucks Company
Flexible Budget Report
For the Second Quarter 20X1

	Actual	Budget	Variance—Favorable/(Unfavorable)
Sales: Expected 17,000 Actual 17,500			
Sales Units	17,500	17,500	0
Sales	$259,000	$262,500	$(3,500)
Cost of Goods Sold	196,875	196,875	0
Gross Profit	62,125	65,625	(3,500)
Selling Expenses	24,610	24,750	140
General and Administrative Expenses	20,250	20,250	0
Operating Income	17,265	20,625	(3,360)
Interest Expense	0	0	0
Income before Income Taxes	17,265	20,625	(3,360)
Income Taxes	6,906	8,250	1,344
Net Income	$ 10,359	$ 12,375	$(2,016)

The flexible budget shows an even higher unfavorable variance than the static budget. This does not always happen but is why flexible budgets are important for giving management an indication of what questions need to be asked.

Preparation of a Flexible Budget

The flexible budget uses the same selling price and cost assumptions as the original budget. Variable and fixed costs do not change categories. The *variable* amounts are recalculated using the actual level of activity, which in the case of the income statement is sales units. Each flexible budget line will be discussed separately.

Sales. The original budget assumed 17,000 Pickup Trucks would be sold at $15 each. To prepare the flexible budget, the units will change to 17,500 trucks, and the actual sales level and the selling price will remain the same. The $262,500 is 17,500 trucks times $15 per truck. The variance that exists now is simply due to price. Given that the variance is unfavorable, management knows the trucks were sold at a price below the $15 budgeted selling price.

Cost of Goods Sold. Using the cost data from the budgeted income statement, the expected total cost to produce one truck was $11.25. The flexible budget cost of goods sold of $196,875 is $11.25 per pick up truck times the 17,500 trucks sold. The lack of a variance indicates that costs in total (materials, labor, and overhead) were the same as planned.

Selling Expenses. The original budget for selling expenses included variable and fixed expenses. To determine the flexible budget amount, the two variable costs need to be updated. The new budget for sales commissions is $10,500 ($262,500 sales times 4%), and the new budget for delivery expense is $1,750 (17,500 units times 10%). These are added to the fixed costs of $12,500 to get the flexible budget amount of $24,750.

General and Administrative Expenses. This flexible budget is unchanged from the original (static budget) because it consists only of fixed costs which, by definition, do not change if the activity level changes.

Income Taxes. Income taxes are budgeted as 40% of income before income taxes. The flexible budget for income before income taxes is $20,625, and 40% of that balance is $8,250. Actual expenses are lower because the income before income taxes was lower. The actual tax rate is also 40%.

Net Income. Total net income changes as the amount for each line on the income statement changes. The net variance in this example is mainly due to lower revenues.

The important thing to remember in preparing a flexible budget is that if an amount, cost or revenue, was variable when the original budget was prepared, that amount is still variable and will need to be recalculated when preparing a flexible budget. If, however, the cost was identified as a fixed cost, no changes are made in the budgeted amount when the flexible budget is prepared. Differences may occur in fixed expenses, but they are not related to changes in activity within the relevant range.

Budget reports can be a useful tool for evaluating a manager's effectiveness only if they contain the appropriate information. When preparing budget reports, it is important to include in the report the items the manager can control. If a manager is only responsible for a department's costs, to include all the manufacturing costs or net income for the company would not result in a fair evaluation of the manager's performance. If, however, the manager is the Chief Executive Officer, the entire income statement should be used in evaluating performance.

Standard Costs

When budgets are prepared, the costs are usually computed at two levels, in total dollars so an income statement can be prepared, and cost per unit. The cost per unit is referred to as a **standard cost**. A standard cost can also be developed and used for pricing decisions and cost control even if a budget is not prepared. A standard cost in a manufacturing company such as Pickup Trucks Company consists of per unit costs for direct materials, direct labor, and overhead. The per unit costs can be further divided into the expected amount and cost of materials per unit, the expected number of hours and cost per hour for direct labor, and the expected total overhead costs and a method for assigning those costs to each unit. Within the expected amount of materials, waste or spoilage must be considered when determining the standard amount. For example, if a product, such as a chair, requires material, more material than is actually needed for the chair must be ordered because the shape of the seat and the fabric are usually not exactly the same. The scraps of material are called waste, which is not avoidable, given that the chair is being produced with this specific fabric. The cost of the full piece of material is used as the standard cost because the waste has no other use.

Similarly, when considering labor hours, downtime from production due to maintenance or start up and break time must be included in the number of hours it takes to make a product. Once standards are established, they are used to analyze and determine the reasons for actual cost variances from standards. The variances may be in quantity of materials or hours used to manufacture a product or in the cost of the materials or labor. Because overhead is normally applied on some basis, the variances in overhead will occur because the total overhead pool of dollars or the activity level (for example, direct labor dollars or hours) used to allocate the overhead is different from what was planned. Once standard costs are used in preparing budgets, analysis of variances can be used to provide management with information about whether a variance is caused by quantity or price so that appropriate action can be taken.

To illustrate how cost variance analysis works, assume you are the plant manager for Bases, Inc., a company that makes a set of soft bases for playing baseball in gymnasiums. The budget assumes 150,000 sets of bases will be produced annually. The following standard cost per set of bases was developed:

	Quantity per set	*Cost*	*Cost per set*
Direct Materials	4.5 feet	$1.10	$ 4.95
Direct Labor	.5 hour	$9 per hour	4.50
Manufacturing Overhead	.5 hour	$1.30 per direct labor hour	.65
Total Cost per Unit			$10.10

The predetermined overhead rate of $1.30 will result in $0.65 of overhead being allocated to each set of bases produced. (It is calculated using .5 direct labor hours per set times $1.30 per hour.)

Bases, Inc.
Manufacturing Overhead Budget
20X1

Production in Units 150,000

Direct Labor Hours per Unit = .5

Direct Labor Hours = 75,000***

	Cost per Direct Labor Hour	Total Cost	Monthly Cost
Variable Costs			
Indirect Materials	$0.02	$ 1,500	*
Indirect Labor	.40	30,000	*
Maintenance	.30	22,500	*
Total Variable Costs	$0.72	54,000	*
Fixed Cost			
Depreciation, Machinery		6,300	$ 525 **
Building Rent		12,000	1,000 **
Supervisor's Salary		25,200	2,100 **
Total Fixed Costs	0.58	43,500	$ 3,625 **
Total Manufacturing Overhead (1)	$1.30	$97,500	
Budgeted Direct Labor Hours (2)		75,000	
Predetermined (standard) Overhead Rate (1) ÷ (2)		$1.30	

* Varies with actual number of units produced.

** One-twelfth of annual fixed costs.

*** Units × .5 hour per unit.

The overhead costs per direct labor hour are:

Variable Costs ($54,000 / 75,000 hours)	$0.72
Fixed Costs ($43,500 / 75,000 hours)	0.58
Total Overhead Cost per Direct Labor Hour	$1.30

For the month of October, the company produced 13,300 sets of bases. The following information was taken from the October financial report.

Direct Materials Purchased and Used (60,000 feet)		$ 63,000
Direct Labor Hours (6,500 hours)		63,375
Overhead		
Variable	$5,330	
Fixed	3,800	
Total Overhead		9,130
Total Actual Product Cost		135,505
Total Standard Product cost (13,300 × $10.10)		134,330
Unfavorable Variance		$ 1,175

Variance Analysis

In order to understand the $1,175 unfavorable monthly variance, it must be analyzed by its component parts: direct materials variances, direct labor variances, and overhead variances. Each of these variances can further be broken down into a price (rate) variance and a quantity (usage or efficiency) variance. A general template that can be used for direct materials variances, direct labor variances, and variable overhead variances uses three amounts — actual, flexible budget, and standard — as a basis for calculating the variances.

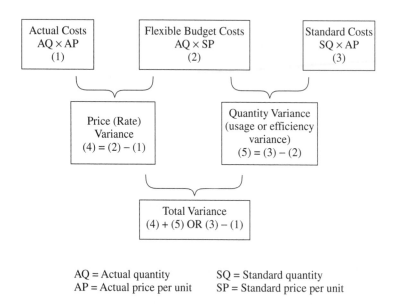

AQ = Actual quantity   SQ = Standard quantity
AP = Actual price per unit SP = Standard price per unit

The price variance is favorable if actual costs are less than flexible budget costs. The quantity variance is favorable if flexible budget costs are less than standard costs. The total variance is favorable if the actual costs are less than standard costs.

Direct Materials Variances

The total direct materials variance is $2,835 favorable and consists of a $3,000 favorable price variance and a $165 unfavorable quantity variance.

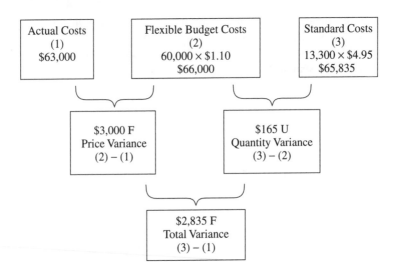

Actual costs of $63,000 are less than flexible budget costs of $66,000, so the materials price variance is $3,000 favorable. The variance can also be thought of on a price per unit basis. The actual costs of $63,000 were for 60,000 feet of direct material, so the actual price per foot is $1.05 ($63,000 ÷ 60,000). The original budget was for a direct materials cost of $1.10 per foot, so it was expected that 60,000 feet of material would cost $66,000. The direct materials actually cost less than budget by $0.05 per foot ($1.10 budget versus $1.05 actual), so the variance is favorable. The direct materials quantity variance of $165 unfavorable means this company used more direct materials than planned because flexible budget costs of $66,000 are higher than the standard costs of $65,825. To produce 13,300 sets of bases, the company expected a cost of $4.95 per set (4.5 feet of material at $1.10 per foot), for a total cost of $65,835. This can also be analyzed by identifying the total feet of material it should have taken to produce 13,300 sets of bases and multiplying by the cost per foot of material (13,300 sets × 4.5 feet per unit = 59,850 feet of direct materials × $1.10 per foot = $65,835). It actually used 60,000 feet, which prices out at an expected $1.10 per foot to be $66,000. The total direct materials variance is calculated by adding the price and quantity variances together or by comparing actual cost of direct materials with the standard cost of producing 13,300 sets of bases.

Another way of computing the direct materials variance is using formulas.

Direct Materials Price Variance = [(AQ × AP) − (AQ × SP)] or AQ(AP − SP)

Direct Materials Quantity Variance = [(AQ × AP) − (AQ × SP)] or AQ(AQ − SQ)

Using the formulas to calculate the variances would work like this:

Direct materials price variance:

$3,000 F	= [(60,000 × $1.05) − (60,000 × $1.10)]	or	60,000($1.05 − 1.10)
$3,000F	= $63,000 − $66,000	or	60,000 × $0.05

Direct materials quantity variance:

$165 U	= [(60,000 × $1.10) − ((13,300 × 4.5) × $1.10)]	or	$1.10(60,000 − (13,300 × 4.5))
$165 U	= ($66,000 − (59,850 × $1.10))	or	$1.10(60,000 − 59,850)
$165 U	= $66,000 − 65,835	or	$1.10 × 150

Once the variances are calculated, management completes the analysis by obtaining explanations for why the variances occurred. For example, a question raised is "Why did materials cost less than planned?" As an answer, management may learn there was a price decrease, or the direct materials were acquired from another source, or lower quality materials were obtained. The explanations for price variances must relate to the *cost* of the direct materials, not the quantity of the materials used. Similarly, the reasons for the quantity variance need to relate to the *amount* of materials used, not the price paid for the materials. Reasons for a quantity variance could be more waste or scrap than was planned, or that lower quality materials were used, or less skilled workers were hired or used on the production line, or machine problems occurred that damaged materials.

Recording direct materials variances. The direct materials price variance is recorded when the direct materials are purchased. The materials are recorded using actual quantity and standard cost. A separate account is used to track each variance.

General Journal

Date	Account and Title Description	Ref.	Debit	Credit
20X1				
Oct.16	Raw Materials Inventory		66,000	
	Direct Materials Price Variance			3,000
	Accounts Payable			63,000
	Record Materials Purchased			

The materials quantity variance is recorded when direct materials are requested by production. Direct materials are taken out of raw materials inventory at the same cost they were put in (actual materials quantity at standard price), and work-in-process inventory is increased based on the units produced at standard cost.

General Journal

Date	Account Title and Description	Ref.	Debit	Credit
20X1				
Oct. 31	Work-in-Process Inventory		65,835	
	Direct Materials Quantity Variance		165	
	Raw Materials Inventory			66,000
	Record Materials Added to Production			

Direct Labor Variances

The total direct labor variance is $3,525 unfavorable and consists of a $4,875 unfavorable rate variance and a $1,350 favorable efficiency variance.

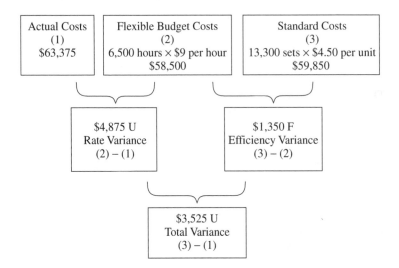

Actual labor costs of $63,375 are more than flexible budget costs of $58,500, so the labor rate variance is $4,875 unfavorable. As with materials, the labor can also be thought of on a price per hour basis. The actual costs of $63,375 were for 6,580 hours, which calculates to an average pay rate of $9.75 per direct labor hour. The budget used a rate of $9.00 per direct labor hour. This $0.75 per hour difference resulted in the unfavorable rate variance because actual costs were higher than budgeted costs. This could result from unplanned but negotiated wage rate increases or the use of a more skilled work force.

The efficiency variance is favorable because flexible costs of $58,500 are less than standard costs of $59,850. This means that the employees took less time than budgeted to produce the 13,300 sets of bases. 13,300 units were produced, and the company expected that the labor cost would be $4.50 per set, for a total labor cost of $59,850. This can also be analyzed by identifying the total hours of labor it should have taken to produce 13,300 sets of bases and multiplying by the cost per hour of labor (13,300 sets × .5 hours = 6,650 hours × $9 per hour = $59,850). Because only 6,500 direct labor hours were needed instead of the 6,650 hours expected, the direct labor efficiency variance is favorable.

The direct labor variances may also be calculated using formulas.

Direct labor rate variance =
$[(AH \times AR) - (AH \times SR)]$ or $AH(AR - SR)$

$4,875 U = [(6,500 \times \$9.75) - (6,500 \times \$9)]$ or $6,500(\$9.75 - \$9)$

$4,875 U = \$63,375 - \$58,500$ or $6,500 \times \$0.75$

Direct labor efficiency (quantity) variance =
$[(AH \times SR) - (SH \times SR)]$ or $SR(AH - SH)$

$1,350 F = [(6,500 \times \$9) - ((13,300 \times .5) \times \$9)]$ or
$\$9(6,500-(13,300 \times .5))$

$1,350 F = (\$58,500 - (6,650 \times \$9))$ or $\$9(6,500 - 6,650)$

$1,350 F = \$58,500 - 59,850$ or $\$9 \times 150$

Recording direct labor variances. The direct labor rate variance is recorded when payroll is accrued.

General Journal

Date	Account Title and Description	Ref.	Debit	Credit
20X1				
Oct. 31	Factory Labor		58,500	
	Direct Labor Rate Variance		4,875	
	Wages Payable			63,375
	Record Direct Labor			

The direct labor efficiency variance is recorded when the direct labor is assigned to work-in-process inventory.

General Journal

Date	Account Title and Description	Ref.	Debit	Credit
20X1				
Oct. 31	Work-in-Process Inventory		59,850	
	Direct Labor Efficiency Variance			1,350
	Factory Labor			58,500
	Assign Direct Labor to Work-in-Process Inventory			

Overhead Variances

Variances may occur for both the variable and fixed cost components of manufacturing overhead. Before looking at the variances, a summary of the overhead information for Bases, Inc., might be helpful. The original plan was for 12,500 units per month, and the actual production for October was 13,300 units.

Bases, Inc.
Manufacturing Overhead
For the Month of October 20X1

	Budgeted Overhead per Direct Labor Hours	Actual (6,500 Direct Labor Hours)	Flexible Budget (6,500 Direct Labor Hours)	Standard (6,650 Direct Labor Hours)	Overhead Applied (6,650 Direct Labor Hours)
Variable Costs					
Indirect Materials	$0.02	$ 390	$ 130	$ 133	
Indirect Labor	.40	2,795	2,600	2,660	
Maintenance	.30	2,145	1,950	1,995	
Total Variable Costs		5,330	4,680	4,788	
Fixed Costs					
Depreciation, machinery		600	525	525	
Building Rent		1,000	1,000	1,000	
Supervisor Salary	.58	2,200	2,100	2,100	
Total Fixed Costs		3,800	3,625 [(2)]	3,625 [(2)]	
Total Overhead Costs	$1.30	$9,130	$8,305	$8,413	$8,645 [(1)]

(1) 13,300 units × $0.65 standard cost per unit (.5 hour × $1.30 predetermined overhead rate).
(2) Budgeted per month.

The variances can be calculated in total for variable and fixed costs, in which case the variances are referred to as the controllable (price) variance and the volume variance. Alternatively, the variances can be calculated separately for variable manufacturing overhead costs and fixed manufacturing overhead costs. The variable overhead cost variances are called the spending (rate) variance and the efficiency variance, and fixed overhead cost variances are known as the spending and volume variances. The variable overhead cost spending variance, the variable overhead cost efficiency variance, and the fixed overhead cost spending variance added together are the same as the controllable variance.

Manufacturing Overhead

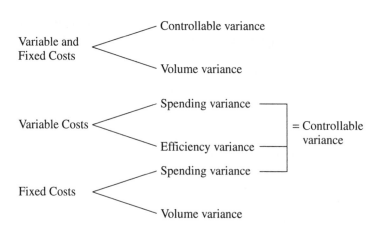

Using the **two-variance approach**, the controllable cost variance shows how well management controls its overhead costs. If a volume variance exists, it means the plant operated at a different production level than budgeted. For the Bases, Inc., the total overhead variance is $485 unfavorable. It consists of a $717 unfavorable controllable variance and a $232 favorable volume variance. An unfavorable controllable variance indicates that overhead costs per direct labor hour were higher than expected. The variance is calculated by subtracting the $8,413 budgeted overhead from the $9,130 actual overhead costs. The budgeted overhead is calculated by adding budgeted variable costs for the actual number of units (think of this as the flexible budget amount) to the budgeted fixed costs (unchanged from original budget).

For Bases, Inc., production was 13,300 units and variable costs were $0.72 per direct labor hour. As each unit takes .5 direct labor hours to make, the variable overhead is 13,300 units times .5 hours times $0.72, or $4,788. When added to fixed costs of $3,625, the total budgeted overhead costs are $8,413 for the month. Possible reasons for the unfavorable variance are: indirect materials were purchased from a different supplier with higher costs, or more indirect materials were used due to waste; indirect labor rates were higher due to a change in personnel or higher negotiated raises than budgeted; and/or fixed overhead costs were more than budgeted.

The $232 volume variance indicates an over-application of fixed costs. This occurred because actual production is higher than the budget. Remember that as more units are produced, fixed costs per unit decrease. However, the predetermined overhead rate is established when the budget is prepared, and the same rate is used throughout the year regardless of the actual number of units produced. So even though the fixed costs per unit decreased when 13,300 units were produced rather than the 12,500 budgeted, the same predetermined overhead rate using the higher cost per unit was used to allocate overhead to production.

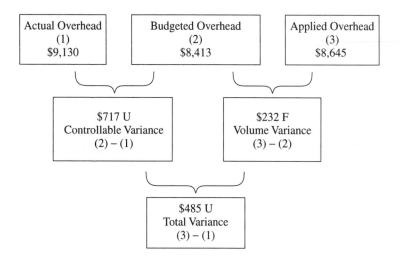

Using the separate overhead variance calculations for variable and fixed costs, the total overhead variance is the same $485 unfavorable. The total variable overhead cost variance is $542 unfavorable, indicating actual variable costs were higher than standard variable costs and, therefore, the overhead is underapplied. The total fixed overhead variance is $57 favorable, indicating overhead is overapplied, because the actual fixed costs are less than the standard fixed costs.

The $650 unfavorable variable cost spending variance is calculated by subtracting the $4,680 flexible budget for variable overhead (actual direct labor hours times variable overhead per direct labor hour, or 6,500 × $0.72) from the actual variable overhead of $5,330. It is unfavorable because more was spent on variable overhead costs per direct labor hour than the $0.72 that was budgeted. Knowing that total variable costs are $5,330 and that 6,500 direct labor hours were incurred, the actual variable overhead costs per direct labor hour rate was $0.82. The $108 favorable efficiency variance is determined by subtracting $4,788 standard overhead (13,300 units by the variable overhead per unit predetermined rate of $0.36) from the flexible budget variable overhead cost of $4,680. It occurred because it took only 6,500 direct labor hours instead of 6,650 (13,300 units × .5 hours per unit) direct labor hours to produce the 13,300 units. The total variable cost variance of $542 is calculated by adding the $650 unfavorable spending variance and the $108 favorable efficiency variance.

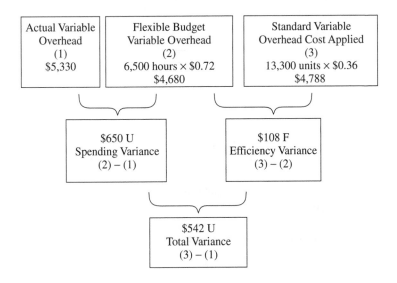

The $175 unfavorable fixed cost spending variance indicates more was spent on fixed costs than was budgeted. It is calculated by subtracting the budgeted fixed overhead per month of $3,625 from the $3,800 actual fixed overhead. The $232 favorable volume variance indicates fixed overhead costs are overapplied. This occurred because there were more units produced than planned. It is calculated by subtracting the applied fixed overhead based on standard cost for units produced of $3,857 (13,300 sets × $0.29 per unit) from budgeted fixed overhead of $3,625. The total fixed overhead cost variance of $57 favorable is the combination of the $175 unfavorable spending variance and the $232 favorable volume variance.

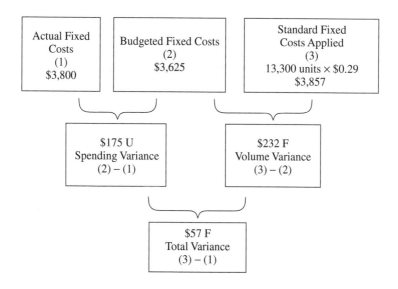

When combined together, the variable overhead spending variance, the variable overhead efficiency variance, and the fixed cost spending variance equal the $717 unfavorable controllable variance calculated under the two-variance method previously discussed.

Recording overhead variances. As manufacturing overhead is incurred, it is recorded in the manufacturing overhead account. The entry to record the variable and fixed components of manufacturing overhead is:

General Journal

Date	Account Title and Description	Ref.	Debit	Credit
20X1				
Oct. 31	Manufacturing Overhead		9,130	
(1)	Raw Materials Inventory (Indirect materials)			390
	Wages Payable (Indirect labor, variable)			2,795
	Maintenance Expense			2,145
	Accumulated Depreciation (depreciation exp.)			600
	Accounts Payable (rent)			1,000
	Wages Payable (Indirect labor, fixed)			2,200
	Record October Overhead Costs			

Manufacturing overhead is applied to production based on direct labor hours.

General Journal

Date	Account Title and Description	Ref.	Debit	Credit
20X1				
Oct. 31	Work-in-Process Inventory (13,300 units ¥ $0.65)		8,645	
(2)	Manufacturing Overhead			8,645
	To Apply Overhead			

At the end of the period, overhead variances are recognized. Under the two variance methods, the entry is:

General Journal

Date	Account Title and Description	Ref.	Debit	Credit
20X1				
Oct. 31	Controllable Variance		717	
(3)	Volume Variance			232
	Manufacturing Overhead			485
	To Record Overhead Variances			

Once these entries are recorded, the manufacturing overhead account is zero.

Manufacturing Overhead

(1)	9,130	8,645	(2)
		485	(3)
	9,130	9,130	
	0		

Using the second method described for manufacturing overhead variances, the entry to record the overhead variances would be:

General Journal

Date	Account Title and Description	Ref.	Debit	Credit
20X1				
Oct. 31	Variable Overhead Costs Spending Variance		650	
	Fixed Overhead Costs Spending Variance		175	
	Variable Overhead Efficiency Variance			108

Date	Account Title and Description	Ref.	Debit	Credit
	Volume Variance			232
	Manufacturing Overhead			485
	Record October Overhead Variances			

Total Variance

The $1,175 total unfavorable variance has now been analyzed into its components for further follow-up by management:

Direct Materials Price Variance	$3,000 F
Direct Materials Quantity Variance	165 U
Direct Labor Price Variance	4,875 U
Direct Labor Quantity Variance	1,350 F
Overhead Controllable Variance	717 U
Overhead Volume Variance	232 F
Total Variance	$1,175 U

The balances in the variance accounts are usually closed to the cost of goods sold account, particularly when the amounts are small. Alternatively, the balances in the variance accounts may be allocated to the appropriate inventory accounts and the cost of goods sold account.

Managerial decisions are choices made based on financial and nonfinancial information. Typically, financial information serves as the first hurdle in identifying a possible course of action as an alternative. If the financial hurdle is met, then management must consider the impact of the alternative on the environment, the company's employees, its image, the community, its partners or alliances, and so on before making a final decision.

Incremental analysis, sometimes called marginal or differential analysis, is used to analyze the financial information needed for decision making. It identifies the relevant revenues and/or costs of each alternative and the expected impact of the alternative on future income.

To illustrate the concept, think about the decision to lease or buy a car. Leasing involves a regular payment and the return of the vehicle at the end of the lease unless a one-time payment is made. This arrangement means the car does not legally belong to the person leasing it. To buy a car requires payment of the purchase price. The payment may be made in cash or by signing a note payable for the amount owed. If you were to prepare financial statements under each alternative, they would look very different. An operating lease for a car with payments of $300 per month would result in the annual cost of the lease, $3,600, being reported as an expense on the income statement. The purchase of a car results in an asset — and a liability, if a note was signed — being recorded on the company's balance sheet.

Another example is the choice between alternatives A and B, given the following relevant revenues and expenses:

	Alternative A	Alternative B	Net Income Increase/ (Decrease)
Revenues	$100,000	$150,000	$50,000
Expenses	78,000	105,000	(27,000)
Net Income	$ 22,000	$ 45,000	$23,000

This example shows alternative B generates $23,000 more net income than alternative A. Management must now consider the non-financial information to determine whether alternative B should be accepted.

Several concepts are incorporated into incremental analysis and need to be defined before discussing some specific applications of incremental analysis.

- **Relevant cost.** Those revenues and costs that differ among alternatives, as opposed to revenues and costs that stay the same, which are ignored when analyzing alternatives. *Note:* Some texts refer to the revenues that change as relevant benefits.

- **Sunk cost.** A cost that has already been incurred and, therefore, has no impact on future decisions because the cost will not change or go away in the future. The book value of a previously purchased and currently owned asset will not change whether or not a new asset is purchased to replace it.

- **Opportunity cost.** A potential benefit that is lost when a company chooses another alternative.

Examples of Incremental Analysis

- Accepting additional business.
- Making or buying parts or products.
- Selling products or processing them further.
- Eliminating a segment.
- Allocating scarce resources (sales mix).

Accepting additional business

The Party Connection prepares complete party kits for various types of celebrations. It is currently operating at 75% of its capacity. It costs The Party Connection $4.50 to make a packet that it sells for $25.00. It currently makes and sells 84,000 packets per year. Detailed information follows:

	Per Unit	*Annual Total*
Sales	$ 25.00	$2,100,000
Direct Materials	12.00	1,008,000
Direct Labor	6.00	504,000
Overhead	.50	42,000
Selling Expenses	1.75	147,000
Administrative Expenses	.25	21,000
Total Costs and Expenses	20.50	1,722,000
Operating Income	$ 4.50	$ 378,000

The Party Connection has received a special order request for 15,000 packets at a price of $20 per packet to be shipped overseas. This transaction would not affect the company's current business. If 84,000 packets is 75% of capacity, 112,000 packets would be 100% of capacity. The Party Connection has the capacity to prepare the 15,000 packets requested without changing its existing operations. Should the Party Connection accept this special order? Using its current cost information, the answer would be no because accepting the order would generate a $7,500 loss.

	Per Unit	*Totals*
Sales	$20.00	$300,000
Direct Materials	12.00	180,000
Direct Labor	6.00	90,000
Overhead	.50	7,500
Selling Expenses	1.75	26,250
Administrative Expenses	.25	3,750
Total Costs and Expenses	20.50	307,500
Operating Income	$ (.50)	$(7,500)

However, this is not the proper way to analyze the alternative. Incremental analysis, which identifies only those revenues and costs that change if the order were accepted, should be used to analyze the alternative. This requires a review of the costs. Suppose the following information is discovered with further analysis:

- Accepting this order would not impact current sales.
- To manufacture 15,000 packets would require $12.00 of direct materials and $6.00 of direct labor.

- The per unit overhead cost of $0.50 is 50% variable ($0.25) and 50% fixed ($0.25).

- Selling costs (includes commissions and delivery costs) for the 15,000 packets would be $7,000.

- Administrative expenses would not change.

	Per Unit	*Totals*
Sales	$ 20.00	$300,000
Direct Materials	12.00	180,000
Direct Labor	6.00	90,000
Overhead	.25	3,750
Selling Expenses		7,000
Total Costs and Expenses		280,750
Operating Income		$ 19,250

Under this scenario, $300,000 of additional revenues would be created with additional costs of $280,750, so operating income would increase by $19,250 if the order were accepted. Given the available capacity, this opportunity would not result in additional costs to expand capacity. If the current capacity were unable to handle the special request, any new costs for expanding capacity would be included in the analysis. Also, if current sales were impacted by this order, then the lost contribution margin would be considered an opportunity cost for this alternative. With additional operating income of $19,250, this order could be accepted.

Making or buying component parts or products

The decision to make or buy component parts also uses incremental analysis to determine the relevant costs. Opportunity costs must also be considered. Toyland Treasures uses part #56 in several of its products. Toyland Treasures currently produces 50,000 of part #56 using $0.30 of direct materials, $0.20 of direct labor, and $0.10 of overhead. The purchase of parts is under review by the company's management. Purchasing has determined it would cost $0.75 per unit to purchase 50,000 of part #56. Should Toyland Treasures continue to make part #56 or should it purchase the part?

The total costs to produce part #56 are $30,000, a savings of $7,500 over the purchase option, and the choice would be for Toyland Treasures to continue to make the part.

	Make	*Buy*	*Incremental Increase/ (Decrease)*
Purchase ($0.75)		$37,500	$(37,500)
Direct Materials ($.30)	$15,000		15,000
Direct Labor ($0.20)	10,000		10,000
Overhead ($0.10)	5,000		5,000
Total Relevant Costs	$30,000	$37,500	$ (7,500)

If Toyland Treasures can use the part #56 production space for a product that would generate $20,000 of additional operating income, the make or buy analysis would generate incremental costs of $12,500 to make the part. In this case, the company would likely choose to purchase part #56 and produce the other product. The $20,000 additional operating income is considered an opportunity cost and is added to the Make column of the analysis.

	Make	Buy	Incremental Increase/ (Decrease)
Total Relevant Costs	$30,000	$37,500	$ (7,500)
Opportunity Cost	20,000		20,000
Total Costs	$50,000	$37,500	$12,500

Selling products or processing further

Some companies' product can be sold at different stages in their production cycle. For example, the DGK Company manufactures children's play gyms. It can sell the gyms assembled or unassembled. Incremental analysis is used in the decision to sell unassembled products. A general guideline DGK should consider when deciding how to sell its units is that if the incremental revenues generated from assembling the gyms are greater than the incremental assembly costs, DGK should assemble the gyms (process further). DGK sells an unassembled gym for $1,000. Its costs to manufacture a gym are $550, which consist of direct materials of $300, direct labor of $150, and overhead of $100. It is estimated that assembling a gym would take additional labor of $100 and overhead of $25, and once assembled, the gym could be sold for $1,500.

	Sell (Unassembled)	Process Further (Assembled)	Operating Income Increase/ (Decrease)
Revenue	$1,000	$1,500	$500
Costs			
Direct Materials	300	300	0

	Sell (Unassembled)	Process Further (Assembled)	Operating Income Increase/ (Decrease)
Direct Labor	150	250	(100)
Overhead	100	125	(25)
Total Costs	550	675	(125)
Operating Income	$ 450	$ 825	$375

On a per unit basis, the incremental analysis shows that DGK should process further and assemble the gyms. Qualitative factors such as loss of business if unassembled gyms were not offered (an opportunity cost) and customers' willingness to pay the additional $500 for an assembled gym need to be considered.

An alternative way of analyzing this decision is:

Sales Price if Process Further (assembled)		$1,500
Sales Price if Sell (unassembled)		1,000
Incremental Revenue		500
Costs to Process Further		
Direct Labor	$100	
Overhead	25	
Total Costs to Process		125
Incremental Operating Income		$ 375

Eliminating an unprofitable segment

If a company has several business segments, one of which is unprofitable, management must decide what to do with the unprofitable segment. In reviewing the quantitative information, a distinction must be made between those costs that will no longer exist if the segment ceases to do business and those costs that will continue and need to be covered by the remaining segments. Costs that go away if the segment no longer operates are called **avoidable costs,** and those that remain even if the segment is discontinued are called **unavoidable costs**.

Segment data for See Me Binoculars, Inc., shows the economy segment has operating income of $120,000, the standard segment has operating income of $250,000, and the deluxe segment is unprofitable by $200,000. The total company has operating income of $170,000.

See Me Binoculars, Inc.
Segment Income Statement
20X0

	Economy	*Standard*	*Deluxe*	*Total*
Revenues	$1,200,000	$1,500,000	$2,500,000	$5,200,000
Variable Expense	900,000	1,000,000	2,200,000	4,100,000
Contribution Margin	300,000	500,000	300,000	1,100,000
Fixed Expenses	180,000	250,000	500,000	930,000
Operating Income	$ 120,000	$ 250,000	$ (200,000)	$ 170,000

To prepare the quantitative analysis for its decision whether to eliminate the deluxe segment, the fixed expenses must be separated into avoidable and unavoidable costs. It has been determined that unavoidable costs will be allocated 45% to economy and 55% to standard. If all the fixed expenses are unavoidable, the company would experience an operating loss of $130,000 if the deluxe segment was discontinued, split as follows:

	Economy	*Standard*	*Total*
Revenues	$1,200,000	$1,500,000	$2,700,000
Variable Expense	900,000	1,000,000	1,900,000
Contribution Margin	300,000	500,000	800,000
Fixed Expenses	405,000*	525,000**	930,000
Operating Loss	$ (105,000)	$ (25,000)	$ (130,000)

* $180,000 + (45\% \times \$500,000)$
** $250,000 + (55\% \times \$500,000)$

    If $300,000 of the fixed expenses are avoidable costs and $200,000 are unavoidable costs, the company's operating income would remain unchanged at $170,000.

	Economy	*Standard*	*Total*
Revenues	$1,200,000	$1,500,000	$2,700,000
Variable Expense	900,000	1,000,000	1,900,000
Contribution Margin	300,000	500,000	800,000
Fixed Expenses	270,000*	360,000**	630,000
Operating Income	$ 30,000	$ 140,000	$ 170,000

*$180,000 + (45\% \times \$200,000)$
**$250,000 + (55\% \times \$200,000)$

The deluxe model has a contribution margin of $300,000, which helps cover some but not all of the fixed expenses generated by its production and the fixed corporate expenses that are allocated to it. If the unavoidable expenses (variable and fixed) are more than the segment's revenues, a decision should be made as to whether to discontinue the segment. If the avoidable expenses are less than the segment's revenues, discontinuing the segment could result in a loss to the company. Although a segment may be unprofitable, it may be contributing to the overall income of the company. This and other factors should be considered before discontinuing the segment.

Allocating scarce resources (sales mix)

When a company sells more than one product and has limited capacity for production of its products, it should optimize its production to produce the highest net income possible. To maximize profit, a calculation of the contribution margin for each product is required. In addition, the amount of the limited capacity each product uses must be determined. For example, if Golfers Paradise produces two different sets of golf clubs, it is limited by its machine capacity of 4,200 hours per month. The relevant data needed to determine production requirements are contribution margin and machine hours required to produce the standard and the deluxe set of golf clubs.

	Standard Set	*Deluxe Set*
Contribution Margin	$150	$270
Machine Hours per Set	.75	1.5

From the relevant data, the deluxe set appears to have the largest contribution margin. However, the standard set can be produced in half the time it takes to produce the deluxe set. To determine which unit should be produced, the contribution margin per hour (the limited resource) must be determined. It is calculated by dividing the contribution margin by the machine hours per set. This calculation shows the standard set has the highest contribution margin when the capacity limitation is considered. The company should produce the standard set.

	Standard Set	Deluxe Set
Contribution Margin	$150	$270
Machine Hours per Set	.75	1.5
Contribution Margin per Hour	$200	$180

If both sets required the same machine hours, the deluxe set would be produced. If the market for the standard set is less than 67,200 (the number of standard sets that could be produced in a year), the deluxe sets should be produced for any excess capacity remaining after the standard sets are produced.

Capital budgeting is the process most companies use to authorize capital spending on long-term projects and on other projects requiring significant investments of capital. Because capital is usually limited in its availability, capital projects are individually evaluated using both quantitative analysis and qualitative information. Most capital budgeting analysis uses cash inflows and cash outflows rather than net income calculated using the accrual basis. Some companies simplify the cash flow calculation to net income plus depreciation and amortization. Others look more specifically at estimated cash inflows from customers, reduced costs, proceeds from the sale of assets and salvage value, and cash outflows for the capital investment, operating costs, interest, and future repairs or overhauls of equipment. One example will be used to illustrate several capital budgeting techniques.

The Cottage Gang is considering the purchase of $150,000 of equipment for its boat rentals. The equipment is expected to last seven years and have a $5,000 salvage value at the end of its life. The annual cash inflows are expected to be $250,000 and the annual cash outflows are estimated to be $200,000.

Capital Budgeting Techniques

Payback Technique
The **payback** measures the length of time it takes a company to recover in cash its initial investment. This concept can also be explained as the length of time it takes the project to generate cash equal to the investment and pay the company back. It is calculated by dividing the capital investment by the net annual cash flow. If the net annual cash flow is not expected to be the same, the average of the net annual cash flows may be used.

$$\text{Cash Payback Period} = \frac{\text{Capital investment}}{\text{Average annual net cash flow}}$$

For the Cottage Gang, the cash payback period is three years. It was calculated by dividing the $150,000 capital investment by the $50,000 net annual cash flow ($250,000 inflows – $200,000 outflows).

$$\frac{\$150,000}{\$50,000} = 3.0 \text{ years}$$

The shorter the payback period, the sooner the company recovers its cash investment. Whether a cash payback period is good or poor depends on the company's criteria for evaluating projects. Some companies have specific guidelines for number of years, such as two years, while others simply require the payback period to be less than the asset's useful life.

When net annual cash flows are different, the cumulative net annual cash flows are used to determine the payback period. If the Turtles Co. has a project with a cost of $150,000, and net annual cash inflows for the first seven years of the project are: $30,000 in year one, $50,000 in year two, $55,000 in year three, $60,000 in year four, $60,000 in year five, $60,000 in year six, and $40,000 in year seven, then its cash payback period would be 3.25 years. See the example that follows.

Year	Expected Net Cash Flows	Cumulative Net Cash Flows
0	$(150,000)	$(150,000)
1	30,000	(120,000)
2	50,000	(70,000)
3	55,000	(15,000) ⎫ *
4	60,000	45,000 ⎭
5	60,000	105,000
6	60,000	165,000
7	40,000	205,000

* Cash payback period is point in time where cumulative net cash
flows equal zero, or 3.25 years in this example.

The cash payback period is easy to calculate but is actually not
the only criteria for choosing capital projects. This method ignores
differences in the timing of cash flows during the project and differences in the length of the project. The cash flows of two projects may
be the same in total but the timing of the cash flows could be very
different. For example, assume project LJM had cash flows of
$3,000, $4,000, $7,000, $1,500, and $1,500 and project MEM had
cash flows of $6,000, $5,000, $3,000, $2,000, and $1,000. Both pro-
jects cost $14,000 and have a payback of 3.0 years, but the cash flows
are very different. Similarly, two projects may have the same payback period while one project lasts five years beyond the payback
period and the second one lasts only one year.

Net present value

Considering the time value of money is important when evaluating projects with different costs, different cash flows, and different service lives. Discounted cash flow techniques, such as the net present value method, consider the timing and amount of cash flows. To use the net present value method, you will need to know the cash inflows, the cash outflows, and the company's required rate of return on its investments. The required rate of return becomes the discount rate used in the net present value calculation. For the calculation in this book, it is assumed that cash flows are received at the end of the period.

Using data for the Cottage Gang and assuming a required rate of return of 12%, the net present value is $80,452. It is calculated by discounting the annual net cash flows and salvage value using the 12% discount factors. The Cottage Gang has equal net cash flows of $50,000 ($250,000 cash receipt minus $200,000 operating costs) so the present value of the net cash flows is computed by using the present value of an annuity of 1 for seven periods. Using a 12% discount rate, the factor is 4.5638 and the present value of the net cash flows is $228,190. The salvage value is received only once, at the end of the seven years (the asset's life), so its present value of $2,262 is computed using the Present Value of 1 table factor for seven periods and 12% discount rate factor of .4523 times the $5,000 salvage value. The investment of $150,000 does not need to be discounted because it is already in today's dollars (a factor value of 1.0000). To calculate the net present value (NPV), the investment is subtracted from the present value of the total cash inflows of $230,452. See the examples that follow. Because the net present value (NPV) is positive, the required rate of return has been met.

Cash Outflows		**Cash Inflows**	
Project Cost	$150,000	Cash from Customers (1)	$250,000
Operating Costs (2)	200,000	Salvage Value	5,000
Estimated Useful Life	7 years		
Minimum Required Rate of Return	12%		
Annual Net Cash Flows ($250,000 – $200,000) (1) – (2)	$50,000		

Present Value of Cash Flows

Annual Net Cash Flows ($50,000 × 4.5638)*	$228,190
Salvage Value ($5,000 × .4523)**	2,262
Total Present Value of Net Cash Inflows	230,452
Less: Investment Cost	(150,000)
Net Present Value	$ 80,452

*Taken from Appendix B.
**Taken from Appendix A.

When net cash flows are not all the same, the Present Value of an Annuity of 1 table cannot be used. Instead, a separate present value calculation must be made for each period's cash flow. A financial calculator or a spreadsheet can be used to calculate the present value. Assume the same project information for the Cottage Gang's investment except for net cash flows, which are summarized with their present value calculations below.

Period	Estimated Annual Net Cash Flow (1)	12% Discount Factor * (2)	Present Value (1) × (2)
1	$ 44,000	.8929	$ 39,288
2	55,000	.7972	43,846
3	60,000	.7118	42,708
4	57,000	.6355	36,224
5	51,000	.5674	28,937
6	44,000	.5066	22,290
7	39,000	.4523	17,640
Totals	$350,000		$230,933

*Taken from Appendix A.

The NPV of the project is $83,195, calculated as follows:

Present Value of Cash Flows

Annual Net Cash Flows	$230,933
Salvage Value ($5,000 × .4523)*	2,262
Total Present Value of Net Cash Inflows	233,195
Less: Investment Cost	(150,000)
Net Present Value	$ 83,195

* Taken from Appendix A.

The difference between the NPV under the equal cash flows example ($50,000 per year for seven years or $350,000) and the unequal cash flows ($350,000 spread unevenly over seven years) is the timing of the cash flows.

Most companies' required rate of return is their **cost of capital**. Cost of capital is the rate at which the company could obtain capital (funds) from its creditors and investors. If there is risk involved when cash flows are estimated into the future, some companies add a risk factor to their cost of capital to compensate for uncertainty in the project and, therefore, in the cash flows.

Most companies have more project proposals than they do funds available for projects. They also have projects requiring different amounts of capital and with different NPVs. In comparing projects for possible authorization, companies use a **profitability index**. The index divides the present value of the cash flows by the required investment. For the Cottage Gang, the profitability index of the project with equal cash flows is 1.54, and the profitability index for the project with unequal cash flows is 1.56.

$$\text{Profitability Index} = \frac{\text{Present Value of Cash Flows}}{\text{Required Investment}}$$

Equal Cash Flows

$$1.54 = \frac{\$230,452}{\$150,000}$$

Unequal Cash Flows

$$1.56 = \frac{\$233,195}{\$150,000}$$

Internal rate of return

The internal rate of return also uses the present value concepts. The internal rate of return (IRR) determines the interest yield of the proposed capital project at which the net present value equals zero, which is where the present value of the net cash inflows equals the investment. If the IRR is greater than the company's required rate of return, the project may be accepted. To determine the internal rate of return requires two steps. First, the internal rate of return factor is calculated by dividing the proposed capital investment amount by the net annual cash inflow. Then, the factor is found in the Present Value of an Annuity of 1 table using the service life of the project for the number of periods. The discount rate that the factor is the closest to is the internal rate of return. A project for Knightsbridge, Inc., has equal net cash inflows of $50,000 over its seven-year life and a project cost of $200,000. By dividing the cash flows into the project investment cost, the factor of 4.00 ($200,000 ÷ $50,000) is found. The 4.00 is looked up in the Present Value of an Annuity of 1 table on the seven-period line (it has a seven-year life), and the internal rate of return of 16% is determined (see Appendix B).

Annual rate of return method

The three previous capital budgeting methods were based on cash flows. The **annual rate of return** uses accrual-based net income to calculate a project's expected profitability. The annual rate of return is compared to the company's required rate of return. If the annual rate of return is greater than the required rate of return, the project may be accepted. The higher the rate of return, the higher the project would be ranked.

The annual rate of return is a percentage calculated by dividing the expected annual net income by the average investment. Average investment is usually calculated by adding the beginning and ending project book values and dividing by two.

$$\text{Annual Rate of Return} = \frac{\text{Estimated Annual Net Income}}{\text{Average Investment}}$$

Assume the Cottage Gang has expected annual net income of $5,572 with an investment of $150,000 and a salvage value of $5,000. This proposed project has a 7.2% annual rate of return ($5,572 net income ÷ $77,500 average investment).

Annual Rate of Return = Estimated Annual Net Income / Average Investment

$$7.2\% = \$5,572 / \$77,500$$

$$(1) \qquad (2)$$

(1) Accrual Basis Income Statement

Revenues	$310,000
Operating Expenses	280,000
Depreciation Expense (A)	20,714
Income before Taxes	9,286
Income Taxes (40%)	3,714
Net Income	$ 5,572

(A) Straight-line with cost of $150,000, salvage value of
$5,000, and a service life of seven years.

$$\frac{\$150,000 - \$5,000}{7}$$

(2) Calculation of Average Investment

Beginning Investment	$150,000
Ending Investment (Salvage Value)	5,000
	155,000
Divide for Average	÷ 2
Average Investment	$ 77,500

The annual rate of return should not be used alone in making capital budgeting decisions, as its results may be misleading. It uses accrual basis of accounting and not actual cash flows or time value of money.

Present Value of 1

Period	2%	4%	5%	6%	8%	10%	12%	14%	16%	18%	20%	22%
1	0.9804	0.9615	0.9524	0.9434	0.9259	0.9091	0.8929	0.8772	0.8621	0.8475	0.8333	0.8197
2	0.9612	0.9246	0.9070	0.8900	0.8573	0.8264	0.7972	0.7695	0.7432	0.7182	0.6944	0.6719
3	0.9423	0.8890	0.8638	0.8396	0.7938	0.7513	0.7118	0.6750	0.6407	0.6086	0.5787	0.5507
4	0.9238	0.8548	0.8227	0.7921	0.7350	0.6830	0.6355	0.5921	0.5523	0.5158	0.4823	0.4514
5	0.9057	0.8219	0.7835	0.7473	0.6806	0.6209	0.5674	0.5194	0.4761	0.4371	0.4019	0.3700
6	0.8880	0.7903	0.7462	0.7050	0.6302	0.5645	0.5066	0.4556	0.4104	0.3704	0.3349	0.3033
7	0.8706	0.7599	0.7107	0.6651	0.5835	0.5132	0.4523	0.3996	0.3538	0.3139	0.2791	0.2486
8	0.8535	0.7307	0.6768	0.6274	0.5403	0.4665	0.4039	0.3506	0.3050	0.2660	0.2326	0.2038
9	0.8368	0.7026	0.6446	0.5919	0.5002	0.4241	0.3606	0.3075	0.2630	0.2255	0.1938	0.1670
10	0.8203	0.6756	0.6139	0.5584	0.4632	0.3855	0.3220	0.2697	0.2267	0.1911	0.1615	0.1369
11	0.8043	0.6496	0.5847	0.5268	0.4289	0.3505	0.2875	0.2366	0.1954	0.1619	0.1346	0.1122
12	0.7885	0.6246	0.5568	0.4970	0.3971	0.3186	0.2567	0.2076	0.1685	0.1372	0.1122	0.0920
13	0.7730	0.6006	0.5303	0.4688	0.3677	0.2897	0.2292	0.1821	0.1452	0.1163	0.0935	0.0754
14	0.7579	0.5775	0.5051	0.4423	0.3405	0.2633	0.2046	0.1597	0.1252	0.0985	0.0779	0.0618

Present Value of 1

Period	2%	4%	5%	6%	8%	10%	12%	14%	16%	18%	20%	22%
15	0.7430	0.5553	0.4810	0.4173	0.3152	0.2394	0.1827	0.1401	0.1079	0.0835	0.0649	0.0507
16	0.7284	0.5339	0.4581	0.3936	0.2919	0.2176	0.1631	0.1229	0.0930	0.0708	0.0541	0.0415
17	0.7142	0.5134	0.4363	0.3714	0.2703	0.1978	0.1456	0.1078	0.0802	0.0600	0.0451	0.0340
18	0.7002	0.4936	0.4155	0.3503	0.2502	0.1799	0.1300	0.0946	0.0691	0.0508	0.0376	0.0279
19	0.6864	0.4746	0.3957	0.3305	0.2317	0.1635	0.1161	0.0829	0.0596	0.0431	0.0313	0.0229
20	0.6730	0.4564	0.3769	0.3118	0.2145	0.1486	0.1037	0.0728	0.0514	0.0365	0.0261	0.0187

Present Value of an Annuity of 1

Period	2%	4%	5%	6%	8%	10%	12%	14%	16%	18%	20%	22%
1	0.9804	0.9615	0.9524	0.9434	0.9259	0.9091	0.8929	0.8772	0.8621	0.8475	0.8333	0.8197
2	1.9416	1.8861	1.8594	1.8334	1.7833	1.7355	1.6901	1.6467	1.6052	1.5656	1.5278	1.4915
3	2.8839	2.7751	2.7232	2.6730	2.5771	2.4869	2.4018	2.3216	2.2459	2.1743	2.1065	2.0422
4	3.8077	3.6299	3.5460	3.4651	3.3121	3.1699	3.0373	2.9137	2.7982	2.6901	2.5887	2.4936
5	4.7135	4.4518	4.3295	4.2124	3.9927	3.7908	3.6048	3.4331	3.2743	3.1272	2.9906	2.8636
6	5.6014	5.2421	5.0757	4.9173	4.6229	4.3553	4.1114	3.8887	3.6847	3.4976	3.3255	3.1669
7	6.4720	6.0021	5.7864	5.5824	5.2064	4.8684	4.5638	4.2883	4.0386	3.8115	3.6046	3.4155
8	7.3255	6.7327	6.4632	6.2098	5.7466	5.3349	4.9676	4.6389	4.3436	4.0776	3.8372	3.6193
9	8.1622	7.4353	7.1078	6.8017	6.2469	5.7590	5.3282	4.9464	4.6065	4.3030	4.0310	3.7863
10	8.9826	8.1109	7.7217	7.3601	6.7101	6.1446	5.6502	5.2161	4.8332	4.4941	4.1925	3.9232
11	9.7868	8.7605	8.3064	7.8869	7.1390	6.4951	5.9377	5.4527	5.0286	4.6560	4.3271	4.0354
12	10.5753	9.3851	8.8633	8.3838	7.5361	6.8137	6.1944	5.6603	5.1971	4.7932	4.4392	4.1274
13	11.3484	9.9856	9.3936	8.8527	7.9038	7.1034	6.4235	5.8424	5.3423	4.9095	4.5327	4.2028
14	12.1062	10.5631	9.8986	9.2950	8.2442	7.3667	6.6282	6.0021	5.4675	5.0081	4.6106	4.2646

Present Value of an Annuity of 1

Period	2%	4%	5%	6%	8%	10%	12%	14%	16%	18%	20%	22%
15	12.8493	11.1184	10.3797	9.7122	8.5595	7.6061	6.8109	6.1422	5.5755	5.0916	4.6755	4.3152
16	13.5777	11.6523	10.8378	10.1059	8.8514	7.8237	6.9740	6.2651	5.6685	5.1624	4.7296	4.3567
17	14.2919	12.1657	11.2741	10.4773	9.1216	8.0216	7.1196	6.3729	5.7487	5.2223	4.7746	4.3908
18	14.9920	12.6593	11.6896	10.8276	9.3719	8.2014	7.2497	6.4674	5.8178	5.2732	4.8122	4.4187
19	15.6785	13.1339	12.0853	11.1581	9.6036	8.3649	7.3658	6.5504	5.8775	5.3162	4.8435	4.4415
20	16.3514	13.5903	12.4622	11.4699	9.8181	8.5136	7.4694	6.6231	5.9288	5.3527	4.8696	4.4603

Notes

Notes

Notes

Notes